A Perfect Redeemer

SERIES EDITORS
Joel R. Beeke & Jay T. Collier

Interest in the Puritans continues to grow, but many people find the reading of these giants of the faith a bit unnerving. This series seeks to overcome that barrier by presenting Puritan books that are convenient in size and unintimidating in length. Each book is carefully edited with modern readers in mind, smoothing out difficult language of a bygone era while retaining the meaning of the original authors. Books for the series are thoughtfully selected to provide some of the best counsel on important subjects that people continue to wrestle with today.

A Perfect Redeemer

William Perkins

Edited by
J. Stephen Yuille

Reformation Heritage Books
Grand Rapids, Michigan

Reformation Heritage Books
3070 29th St. SE
Grand Rapids, MI 49512
616-977-0889
orders@heritagebooks.org
www.heritagebooks.org

Originally published as two treatises: *The True Gain: More in Worth than All the Goods in the World* (1601) and *A Declaration of the True Manner of Knowing Christ Crucified* (1596).

Printed in the United States of America
24 25 26 27 28 29/10 9 8 7 6 5 4 3 2 1

Library of Congress Cataloging-in-Publication Data

Names: Perkins, William, 1558-1602, author. | Yuille, J. Stephen, 1968- editor. |
   Perkins, William, 1558-1602. True gain. | Perkins, William, 1558-1602.
   Declaration of the true manner of knowing Christ crucified.
Title: A perfect redeemer / William Perkins ; edited by J. Stephen Yuille.
Description: Grand Rapids, Michigan : Reformation Heritage Books, [2024] | Series: Puritan treasures for today | "Originally published as two treatises: The True Gain: More in Worth than All the Goods in the World (1601) and A Declaration of the True Manner of Knowing Christ Crucified (1596)." | Includes bibliographical references.
Identifiers: LCCN 2024023676 (print) | LCCN 2024023677 (ebook) |
   ISBN 9798886861372 (paperback) | ISBN 9798886861389 (epub)
Subjects: LCSH: Christian life—Early works to 1800. | Christian life—Puritan authors.
Classification: LCC BV4501.3 .P454 2024 (print) | LCC BV4501.3 (ebook) | DDC
   232/.3—dc23/eng/20240611
LC record available at https://lccn.loc.gov/2024023676
LC ebook record available at https://lccn.loc.gov/2024023677

Table of Contents

Preface

How can sinners be righteous in God's sight? Is there a more important question than this? The answer is by grace *alone* through faith *alone* in Christ *alone*. In a word, Christ does it all. He achieves righteousness in His obedience, and He satisfies God's offended justice by His death upon the cross. The implication is that we are completely passive. We simply receive Christ through faith and, as a result, we "become the righteousness of God in Him" (2 Cor. 5:21). That is exceedingly good news!

But what happens if we add something to this good news? Intentionally or not, we end up denying the sole sufficiency of Christ. "What this means in practice is spelled out in what we can call...theological mathematics...whenever you add, you subtract. Adding more to the Lord Jesus makes Him less than He should be. Whenever you put a plus sign after Jesus, you are taking something away from His supremacy and sufficiency."[1]

Are we convinced of Christ's sole sufficiency? He became one with us in our humanity. "He stripped Himself of the robes of His glory," says Thomas Watson, "and covered Himself with the rags of our humanity."[2] Because He is related to us, He can act as our Redeemer. He "was delivered up because of our offenses, and was raised because of our justification" (Rom. 4:25). He paid the penalty for our sin on the cross, and God testified to His acceptance of Christ's sacrifice by raising Him from the dead. Christ's work, therefore, is enough to atone for our sin, to secure God's forgiveness, and to reconcile us to God. "For Christ also suffered once for sins, the just for the unjust, that He might bring us to God" (1 Peter 3:18).

Are we convinced that God offers Christ to sinners for their salvation? We do not need to fulfill any conditions. We do not need to get our act together or meet a certain standard of behavior. We do not need to be sorry enough, ashamed enough, good enough, or holy enough. We simply need to receive God's offer. We echo Horatius Bonar's cry, "Upon a life I did not live, upon a death I did not die, another's life, another's

---

1. Allan Chapple, *True Devotion: In Search of Authentic Spirituality* (London: The Latimer Trust, 2014), 31.

2. Thomas Watson, *A Body of Divinity* (1692; repr., Edinburgh: Banner of Truth, 1958), 196–98.

death, I stake my whole eternity!"[3] It is important to remind ourselves of God's free offer of Christ because a spirit of legalism lurks in each of us. Deep down, we are convinced that there is something we must do that will make the difference between heaven and hell. Yet, Paul makes it clear that "those who are in the flesh cannot please God" (Rom. 8:8). Our only hope is to look away from ourselves to Christ who has done all. The gospel is not a work to be performed, but a message to be received.

Are we convinced that we receive God's gift (Christ) through faith? When we realize we are physically sick, we look for a doctor. Similarly, when we realize we are spiritually sick, we look for a Savior. This means that Christ is sweet when sin is bitter. When we see our sinfulness before a holy God, we extend the hand of our soul to receive Christ as ours. Having become one with Him, we take possession of all the benefits and blessings that are found in Him. To be united to Christ is justification, adoption, reconciliation, and sanctification. He is indeed an all-sufficient Savior.

What a comforting truth! When we see Christ's sole sufficiency, we see God's steadfast love. "In this is love, not that we loved God, but that He loved us and sent His Son to be the propitiation for our sins" (1 John 4:10). Because of His love, He left a glorious

---

3. Horatius Bonar, "Upon a Life I Have Not Lived" (hymn).

crown and walked in our flesh. Because of His love,
He was hungry, thirsty, and weary. Because of His love,
He was sorrowful unto death. Because of His love, He
was betrayed, arrested, and condemned. Because of
His love, He was crowned with thorns, scourged with
whips, and pierced with nails. Because of His love, He
hung on a shameful cross, bearing our guilt. Because
of His love, He "poured out His soul unto death"
(Isa. 53:12). Christ's crucifixion is the public display of
God's love for us. He is our most loving Father. John
Owen writes, "Every other discovery of God, without this, will but make the soul flee from him; but if
the heart is much taken up with the eminency of the
Father's love, it cannot choose but be overpowered,
conquered, and endeared unto him....Exercise your
thoughts upon this very thing, the eternal, free, and
fruitful love of the Father, and see if your heart is not
wrought upon to delight in him."[4]

What a compelling truth! When we see Christ's
sole sufficiency, we are strengthened to change. "Christ
took our misery that we might have his glory," says
Thomas Manton.[5] This realization compels us to love
Him and out of love to obey Him. Elsewhere, Paul
declares that nothing can separate us from God's love

---

4. John Owen, *Communion with the Triune God*, eds. Kelly Kapic
and Justin Taylor (repr., 1657; Wheaton: Crossway, 2007), 128.

5. Thomas Manton, *The Works of Thomas Manton*, 22 vols., (Bir-
mingham: Solid Ground Christian Books, 2008), 3:266.

in Christ (Rom. 8:31–39). Separation means division (or divorce), but Christ never divorces His bride. Our union with Him is eternal because it is founded upon a love that is eternal and unchangeable. We can rest assured that His love for us does not depend on anything in us. As a matter of fact, we spoil His love when we think it is induced by anything in us. R. C. Sproul explains, "God does not love us because we are lovely. He loves us because Christ is lovely. He loves us in Christ."[6] He loves us because we are one with His beloved Son. As the Holy Spirit impresses this wonderful truth upon us, our love for God grows, and correspondingly, our desire to know and obey His will.

When Christ's sole sufficiency embraces the soul, we proclaim with Paul, "God forbid that I should boast except in the cross of our Lord Jesus Christ, by whom the world has been crucified to me, and I to the world" (Gal. 6:14). When we boast in the cross, we are saying that Christ does it all. He takes our sin, and He achieves righteousness in His obedience. We simply receive Him (and all His benefits) through faith, singing, "Nothing in my hand I bring, simply to the cross I cling."[7] Faith does nothing. It pays nothing, earns nothing, and contributes nothing. It simply receives.

---

6. R. C. Sproul, *Loved by God* (Nashville: Word Publishing, 2001), 35.

7. Augustus Toplady, "Rock of Ages, Cleft for Me" (hymn).

Do we believe in Christ's sole sufficiency? Do we believe that He was crucified for us—that He stood in our place while our sins were applied to Him? As we hear of Christ agonizing in the garden, do we think of our sins that brought such pain upon Him? As we hear of Christ's condemnation before Pilate, do we marvel at God's infinite mercy toward sinners? As we hear of Christ naked upon the cross, do we remember that He covers our shame with His righteousness? As we hear of Christ's cry from the cross, do we think of how He suffered the torment of hell in our place? As we hear of the trembling of the earth, do we think of how we deserved to descend to hell? This is to believe in an all-sufficient Savior.

There is nothing more soul satisfying than contemplating our interest in Christ. And this is what makes the present volume so compelling.[8] Here William Perkins (1558–1603) offers an insightful treatment of what it means to rest in Christ's sole sufficiency. In his preaching of the gospel, Perkins repeatedly

---

8. This book abridges and combines two of William Perkins's smaller (and lesser known) treatises. Chapters 1–20 are taken from *The True Gain: More in Worth than All the Goods in the World* (1601) and chapters 21–27 from *A Declaration of the True Manner of Knowing Christ Crucified* (1596). They are found in *The Works of William Perkins*, ed. J. Stephen Yuille (Grand Rapids: Reformation Heritage Books, 2020), 9:1–78. The conclusion is taken from Perkins, *Christ's Sermon on the Mount*, in *The Works of William Perkins*, ed. J. Stephen Yuille (Grand Rapids: Reformation Heritage Books, 2014) 1:718–19.

emphasized two fundamental truths: Christ's atoning death whereby He bore the wrath of God in our place, and Christ's perfect life whereby He fulfilled all righteousness on our behalf. When explaining "the very thing for which a sinner is justified," he insisted that "it is the obedience of Christ, the Redeemer and Mediator, passive and active."[9] We become partakers of His obedience through faith in Him. "As mutual love joins one man to another," says Perkins, "so true faith makes us one with Christ."[10] This union is our knitting together with Christ, our engrafting into Him, our eating of His flesh, our drinking of His blood, and our joining into His body. It is by means of this union that "Christ, with all His benefits, is made ours."[11] Consequently, we enjoy a new legal status and identity in Him. Moreover, we have communion with Him in His names and titles; we have communion with Him in His righteousness; we have communion with Him in His death and resurrection; and we have communion with Him in His glory.

Here William Perkins is at his finest, as he extols the surpassing excellence of the knowledge of Jesus Christ.

---

9. Perkins, *Jude*, 27.

10. William Perkins, *Christ's Sermon on the Mount*, in *The Works*, 1:718.

11. William Perkins, *A Golden Chain*, in *The Works of William Perkins*, eds. Joel R. Beeke and Greg A. Salazar (Grand Rapids: Reformation Heritage Books, 2018), 6:183.

As you read, may your faith be strengthened, your hope renewed, and your love inflamed! May you grow in your appreciation of what it means to rest in "a perfect Christ, a perfect Redeemer!"[12]

J. Stephen Yuille
Fort Worth, TX

---

12. William Perkins, *A Godly and Learned Exposition Upon the Whole Epistle of Jude*, ed. J. Stephen Yuille (Grand Rapids: Reformation Heritage Books, 2017), 4:57.

Introduction

It is a conclusion of our religion, worthy of careful consideration, that Jesus Christ alone is our Mediator, Justifier, Redeemer, and Savior, by works and merits which He produced by Himself, and not by any works or merits which He produces in us by the Holy Spirit.

The Scripture confirms it in express words. We are "justified freely by His grace through the redemption that is in Christ Jesus" (Rom. 3:24). "For He made Him who knew no sin to be sin for us, that we might become the righteousness of God in Him" (2 Cor. 5:21). We "have put on the new man who is renewed in knowledge according to the image of Him who created him" (Col. 3:10). "When He had by Himself purged our sins, [He] sat down at the right hand of the Majesty on high" (Heb. 1:3). "With His own blood He entered the Most Holy Place once for all, having obtained eternal redemption" (Heb. 9:12). "How much more shall the blood of Christ, who through the eternal Spirit offered Himself without spot to God, cleanse your conscience from dead works to serve the living God?" (Heb. 9:14).

Common reason also testifies to the conclusion that Christ alone is our Mediator, Justifier, Redeemer, and Savior by His works and merits, not our own. If we were able to merit eternal life based on the good works we perform by the Holy Spirit, then we would be partners with Christ, meaning we would participate with Him in the work of our redemption. But such a thing can never be! In reconciling us to God, Christ has no partner.

As the apostle Paul proclaims, "But what things were gain to me, these I have counted loss for Christ. Yet indeed I also count all things loss for the excellence of the knowledge of Christ Jesus my Lord, for whom I have suffered the loss of all things, and count them as rubbish, that I may gain Christ and be found in Him" (Phil. 3:7–9).

The context of Paul's words is his admonition to the Philippians to take heed of counterfeit apostles who join Christ and circumcision as the cause of their salvation, and as a result place their confidence in the flesh—that is, in the outward works of the law (v. 2). He proceeds to explain that it is foolishness to trust in "the works of the law" for salvation because true "circumcision" consists of worshiping God in the Spirit, rejoicing in Christ, and placing no confidence in the flesh (v. 3). Paul is living proof of this. No one had more reason to trust in the flesh than he did (vv. 4–6), yet even he counted the works of the law to be "loss for Christ" (v. 7).

The meaning of Paul's declaration rests on four observations.

First, he speaks of the past, "I have counted loss for Christ" (v. 7), and the present, "I also count all things loss" (v. 8). The first refers to the time prior to his conversion—before he was called to the knowledge of Christ, while the second refers to the time after his conversion, namely, his present ministry as an apostle of Christ.

Second, the English translation, "I also count all things loss" (v. 8), does not fully express the meaning of the Holy Spirit. The words are better translated, "I have made all things loss," or "I have cast away all things," or "I have deprived myself of all things for Christ." In verse 7, Paul says, "I have counted loss for Christ." In verse 8, he intends to amplify his meaning by declaring, "I deprive myself of all things, and judge them to be rubbish in comparison to Christ."

Third, the word "rubbish" is important. The original term signifies something unpleasant such as the entrails of an animal. They are unfit for human consumption, and therefore thrown to the dogs. By using this term, Paul is indicating that he did not only esteem all things as loss and deprive himself of them, but that he cast them away with loathing, and that he was determined to have nothing more to do with them.

Fourth, the similitude in the verse is borrowed from a merchant. In hope of treasure, the merchant is willing to esteem his commodities as loss. He is content to cast them into the sea, and to value them as things that are given to dogs, so that he may obtain his desired treasure. Similarly, Paul says he is willing to count all his former privileges as loss, and he is content to deprive himself of them, to loathe them as rubbish, so that he might obtain Christ.

It is evident that the substance of Paul's words lies in this comparison between his loss ("all things") and his gain ("Christ"). In a word, he considers all things as loss in comparison to Christ. For Paul, this conclusion is an infallible truth, which tears down all self-righteousness and extols the riches of God's grace.

CHAPTER 1

Mercy Alone

But what things were gain to me, these I have counted loss for Christ.
—Philippians 3:7

Let us search carefully into the meaning of these words. To begin with, what are the "things" that Paul considered "gain" before Christ saved him? First, his privileges: he was a Jew, he was circumcised on the eighth day, and he was raised in the strict sect of the Pharisees (v. 5). Second, his virtues: he was zealous in his religion and blameless in his righteousness (v. 6). Third, his works: he observed the moral and ceremonial law. Paul calls these things "gain" because he put his confidence in them, and he thought he could merit eternal life by them.

But the moment arrived when Paul "counted" all these things to be "loss." As soon as he discovered "the excellence of the knowledge of Christ Jesus," his self-confidence dissipated (cf. Rom. 7:9). He realized that all the things which he had formerly viewed as meritorious in God's sight were without any merit at all. They were worthless. And so, he cast them away, so that he might "gain" Christ and "be found" in Him (vv. 7–9).

Paul's declaration teaches us several noteworthy lessons.

First, it was a heresy of the Pharisees to put their confidence in their works and to think that they could merit eternal life by them. As a Pharisee, Paul thought his works were his advantage in the cause of his salvation, but he was mistaken. From his example, we learn what to think of any religion that teaches that we can merit salvation by trusting in our works. Those in the Church of Rome are the children of the old Pharisees, in that they revive and renew the old heresy with new and fresh colors. They attempt to refute this charge by claiming that they ascribe merit to the works of the moral law (not the ceremonial law), and to works of grace (not nature). But the Pharisees made the same claim. The Pharisee acknowledges this very thing in his prayer: "God, I thank You that I am not like other men" (Luke 18:11). What was it that he believed set him apart from other men but his own works—even those for which he thanked God?

Second, it is pride that causes people to desire to be something in themselves, to look to something in themselves as their righteousness before God, and to trust in it as a means of salvation. Habakkuk proclaims, "Behold the proud, his soul is not upright in him" (Hab. 2:4). It was such pride that caused the Jews to seek "to establish their own righteousness," while refusing to submit themselves "to the righteousness of God" (Rom. 10:3). It is not surprising that, in the cause of their salvation, people want to add something of their own merit to the work of Christ, for fallen human nature insists upon something of its own as being meritorious in God's sight. It is little wonder that so many people live and die in the hope of justification by their works. Therefore, let us learn to detect and detest our own pride. Wherever it reigns supreme, Christ is not truly acknowledged. But when we begin to know Christ, our hidden pride soon gives way.

Third, no privileges outside of Christ can impart true comfort and happiness. It is indeed a privilege to eat and drink in Christ's presence (Luke 13:26), yet it is possible to do so without knowing Him. On the day of judgment, He will say to many, "I do not know you, where you are from. Depart from Me, all you workers of iniquity" (v. 27). It is a privilege to be one of Christ's earthly family (Mark 3:32), yet it is ultimately of no real significance, for He says, "Who is My mother or My brothers?...For whoever does the will of God is My brother and My sister and mother" (vv. 33, 35). It is a privilege to be the mother of Christ (Luke 1:42), but if Mary had not carried Him in her heart by faith as she carried Him in her womb, she would not have been saved (vv. 46–55). It is a privilege to prophesy in Christ's name (Matt. 7:22), yet it should not be confused with knowing Him. Again, on the day of judgment, He will say to many, "I never knew you; depart from Me, you who practice lawlessness" (v. 23). It is a privilege to be endued with all kinds of wisdom and learning, and to be able to speak with the tongues of men and angels (1 Cor. 13:1–3), yet it is all worthless and we are "nothing" in God's sight unless we are found in Christ.

This being the case, we must learn to moderate our care and affection for worldly profit, honor, and pleasure. Our principal care must be focused on Christ. Those who live an honest and respectful life, showing love for God and neighbor in outward duties, resting in the fact that they are not thieves, murderers, adulterers, or blasphemers, must be careful not to deceive themselves by building upon false grounds. Though these things are commendable before others, they are insufficient to save us before God. Paul was a strict observer of the law, but after he came to the knowledge of Christ, he counted all his obedience, in which he had formerly trusted, to be nothing more than rubbish.

Fourth, it is a false doctrine of the Church of Rome that, before a man can be justified in Christ, he must prepare and dispose himself to receive his justification. It teaches that when he is sufficiently disposed, he merits that God should infuse righteousness to him whereby he is made righteous before Him. But those who hold to such a doctrine are mistaken. When such a person performs these so-called works of preparation, is he in Christ or out of Christ? If he is in Christ, then he is already justified. If he is out of Christ, then Paul's conclusion is the final word. He says that such works are of no use to commend us to God. Rather, they are to be esteemed as loss, as that which is fit only for dogs.

Fifth, those who would truly come to Christ and receive Him must consider all things to be loss. They must be emptied of all self-righteousness. In a shipwreck people cast their possessions overboard, and when there is no hope for the ship, they jump into the water and swim to shore. Similarly, we must forsake all and then come to Christ. We must lay aside all thoughts of our own goodness. We must be made nothing in ourselves. It is impossible to enter the kingdom of heaven unless we receive Christ as a little child in all meekness and humility. There must be nothing in us to receive Christ but faith alone resting on mercy alone.

CHAPTER 2

The Courtroom of Mercy

Yet indeed I also count all things loss for the excellence of the knowledge of Christ Jesus my Lord.
—Philippians 3:8

We now come to consider those things which Paul considered "loss" after his conversion. In the preceding verse, he says, "what things were gain to me, these I have counted loss for Christ" (v. 7). He knows that, upon hearing this, some people might accuse him of being too rash in his judgment. To avoid this criticism, he declares, "Yet indeed I also count all things loss" (v. 8). That is, "I am not speaking rashly. I say that even now I count all things loss. I say it confidently, and I am resolved in what I say."

When he says, "I count," he is referring to the present time as he is a Christian and an apostle of Christ. When he says, "all things," he is speaking generally. He means everything except his knowledge of and faith in Christ. It includes the privilege of being an apostle. It also includes all Christian virtues such as hope, fear, love, etc. It includes all works of grace, effected by the Holy Spirit in him. Paul says that all these things are his loss for Christ.

How are they loss? Paul's words must be considered carefully. These things are not loss in respect of a godly life, for they are the causes of such a life, and they are the means through which we show our thankfulness to God and our love for our neighbor. When Paul says they are loss, he means in respect of salvation and justification. We do not esteem these things as meritorious causes of salvation, in whole or in part. When they are rightly used and applied, they are the excellent gifts of God. But when they are brought into the act of salvation and justification, they become as loss and rubbish. The prophet Isaiah declares, "And all our righteousnesses are like filthy rags" (Isa. 64:6). Paul says to the Galatians, "If righteousness comes through the law, then Christ died in vain" (Gal. 2:21). That is, if the righteousness of the law is our gain, then Christ must be our loss. On the contrary, if Christ is our gain, then the righteousness of the law must be our loss.

In sum, Paul's point is that all virtues and works (both of nature and grace) are "loss" in the cause of our salvation. Those who are without Christ recoil at such a notion, and they make numerous objections.

Some insist that God accepts and crowns their works, and therefore they are not loss. My answer is that we must remember that God has two courtrooms: one of justice and one of mercy. In the courtroom of justice,

He judges by the law, and He curses "everyone who does not continue in all things which are written in the book of the law, to do them" (Gal. 3:10). The only thing that can stand in this courtroom is the suffering and righteousness of Christ. Rather than looking to be accepted or rewarded for our best works, we ought to cry with David, "Do not enter into judgment with Your servant, for in Your sight no one living is righteous" (Ps. 143:2). In the courtroom of mercy, God deals with His children as they stand before Him justified and reconciled in Christ. He mercifully accepts us and rewards us for our obedience, not for its merit (for it is imperfect), but for the merit of Christ. Thus, we see that, according to God's justice, good works are worthy of condemnation, but according to God's mercy, because they are procured by the merit of Christ, good works are accepted.

Others insist that works are necessary to salvation, and therefore not to be reputed as loss.

My answer is that we must differentiate between works as a cause of salvation and works as a way that leads to final salvation. If they are considered as a cause of salvation, then they are not necessary. In this respect, they are "rubbish." However, if they are viewed as a way that leads and directs to eternal life, they are indeed necessary.

Still others object that the law requires works and it must be satisfied, and therefore he who is justified must be justified by works.

My answer is that we must make a distinction when we speak of works. First, some works are performed by us. They do not save or justify anyone, but in the cause of salvation they are loss and rubbish. Second, some works are performed by Christ—namely the works of obedience in satisfying and fulfilling the law. They are indeed the works that save and justify us. To this effect, Paul says that we are "justified freely by His grace through the redemption that is in Christ Jesus" (Rom. 3:24).

Finally, some say that if all virtues are loss for Christ, then faith itself is loss because it is a virtue.

My answer is that we must consider faith in two ways. First, it must be considered as a virtue working and producing good fruit in us. In this sense, it is to be reputed loss as all other virtues are. Second, it must be considered, not as a virtue, but as an instrument by which we receive and apprehend Christ and His benefits. In this sense, it does not give or work anything, and therefore it is no loss.

We see, therefore, that Paul's doctrine is clear—all works and all virtues (of nature and grace) are loss in the cause of our salvation and justification. Three key lessons emerge from his doctrine.

First, we learn that the holiest works of the holiest people cannot merit eternal life. When such works are introduced as a cause in the act of justification, Paul says that they are as animal entrails to be cast to dogs. Let this be remembered when we are tempted to rest in our own righteousness.

Second, we learn that we are saved and justified by faith alone. All things, except our knowledge of and faith in Christ, are as rubbish. Because this doctrine may be scandalous to some, we must keep several things in mind. The first is that there is nothing in us that is a cause of justification. The second is that faith is not an efficient cause of justification, but only an instrument. The third is that faith is not an instrument to procure our salvation and justification, but simply an instrument to receive our justification which is given by the Father, procured by the Son, and applied by the Holy Spirit. The fourth is that faith must be understood as an instrumental cause of salvation or a way to salvation. As the first, it alone justifies us and saves us. As the second, it does not save us, but is one of many virtues and works which mark the way that leads to eternal life.

Many people object when we say that we are saved by faith alone. They fail to consider faith in two ways. First, faith is an instrument. As such, it does not merit anything, but simply apprehends pardon in Christ and applies it to us for our eternal happiness. Second, faith is a way in which we are to walk for the attainment of eternal life. In the first sense, faith alone saves and justifies, and nothing else. Basil says, "This is perfect rejoicing in God, when a man is not puffed up for his own righteousness, but acknowledges that he lacks righteousness, and that he is justified by faith alone in Christ."[1] But if we speak of the way to life, then we are not saved by faith alone. Though faith is the only instrument to apprehend Christ, it is not the only way to life. Repentance is also the way. All virtues and works are the way. Abraham's faith was not alone but cooperated with his works (James 2:22), because both faith and works are considered a way to happiness or marks in that way.

Third, we learn that the foundation of true humility is that all our virtues and works are loss in the cause of our salvation. The truth that salvation is in Christ alone excludes all boasting. In the matter of our salvation, we are to claim nothing but our sin and shame, and we are to give all the glory to God. If we place any confidence in our works and virtues, the greater will be our eternal loss.

---

1. Basil (AD 330–379) was an import theologian in the early church. He served as bishop of Caesarea in Cappadocia (modern-day Turkey).

CHAPTER 3

God Crowns His Own Grace

Yet indeed I also count all things loss for the excellence of the knowledge of Christ Jesus my Lord, for whom I have suffered the loss of all things, and count them as rubbish, that I may gain Christ.
—Philippians 3:8

We have seen what things Paul considers to be loss. Next, let us consider how they are loss to him. In this verse Paul declares it by way of a gradation: "I counted all things loss...I have suffered the loss of all things... and count them as rubbish." A gradation is a repetition of the same thing in enlarged and amplified words. It usually signifies a thing's certainty and necessity. In our verse Paul's repetition points to the certainty and the necessity of his loss.

Paul's loss of all these things is a certainty for the simple reason that salvation is in Christ alone. Given Christ's sole sufficiency, works (before and after salvation) are without merit. How do we know this?

First, a principal part of a Christian's inherent righteousness is to get and keep a good conscience (1 Tim. 1:19). But Paul expressly excludes a good conscience from justification, saying, "I know nothing against myself, yet I am not justified by this; but He who judges me is the Lord" (1 Cor. 4:4). Therefore, keeping a good conscience is a work without merit.

Second, a Christian is "created in Christ Jesus for good works, which God prepared beforehand that we should walk in them" (Eph. 2:10). But Paul quickly adds that we are not saved by such works (v. 9). Even those works which follow faith, and are performed by the Holy Spirit, are without merit in the cause of our salvation.

Third, a work must please God before it can have any merit. But before a work pleases God, the person who does the work must please Him. But before the person who does the work pleases God, he must be reconciled to Him and justified before Him. Justification, therefore, goes before good works, and works cannot be brought into the act of justification as a cause. Good works do not make good people in whole or in part. Rather, we are first made good by the imputed goodness of Christ, and then by this goodness we do good works.

Fourth, the humanity of Christ is the most excellent of all creatures in heaven and earth, yet, considered by itself, it cannot merit anything at God's hand. There are three conditions that make a work meritorious: (1) the person must do the work by himself, for praise is only due to the person who does it; (2) the work must not be done as a debt or duty; if it is, the person who does the work deserves nothing; (3) there must be a proportion between the work and the reward of eternal life. The humanity of Christ, considered by itself, cannot perform these three conditions. For starters, it does all that it does by the Holy Spirit, by whom it was conceived and was filled without measure. Moreover, it is a creature, and therefore it owes all that it is, all that it has, and all that it can be, to God. Lastly, it cannot do a work proportionate to eternal glory because it receives everything from God and can give nothing to Him.

That said, some might wonder how the humanity of Christ merits on our behalf. The answer is that Christ's humanity is not by itself, but by means of the personal union it is exalted into the unity of the second person, the eternal Word of the Father (John 1:14). That is how Christ merits. No one can merit anything from God but God. Christ alone merits because He alone is God and man. Thus, no mere creature (human or angel) can possibly merit by any work.

Fifth, there are two kinds of transgression. The first is when a person does something directly against the law. The second is when a person does what the law requires, but not in the manner the law requires (which is perfection). This is the case with all good works. No one performs good works in the perfect manner that the law requires. Hence, all good works are a transgression in this respect. Where there is a transgression, there must be pardon. Where there is pardon, there is obviously no merit.

To help us understand the certainty of our loss of all things, let us consider the two chief grounds of merit in which people often trust.

First, they claim the merit of their own works because of the promise that God makes to our works. In short, He says that He will reward them with eternal glory (Rom. 2:6–7).

My response is that they fail to understand that God's promise is made according to His good pleasure, and it is by His goodness that a person does any good work by nature or grace. Therefore, if a person could fulfill the whole law, he would still not merit anything at God's hand. The Lord says that He shows "mercy to thousands, to those love [Him] and keep [His] commandments" (Ex. 20:6).

Second, they claim the merit of their own works because of the supposed virtue that is derived from Christ, the Head of the body, to His members by divine influence.

My response is that their reasoning is faulty. The virtue of meriting is in Christ, not simply as He is man, but as He is God and man in one person. The work that merits is done by His manhood, but the merit of the work is from His Godhead, or from the excellence of His person. If this virtue is in Christ, not as He is a man, but in respect of the fact that He is God and man, it cannot be derived to us who are but human, unless we should be deified, which is impossible. Therefore, there is no possibility of merit in a person's works.

For this cause, the true church of God has always rejected any notion of human merit. Augustine[1] writes, "God crowns only His own grace in us." He adds, "No man may think that God is bound (as it were) by a bargain to repay that which He has promised. As God is free to promise, so He is free in respect of repaying, especially considering that merits as well as rewards are His grace. God crowns nothing else in us but His grace. If He should deal with us in any other way, no one could be justified in His sight." For his part, Anslem[2] says, "If a man should serve God a thousand years, and do so most zealously, he would not deserve to be in the kingdom of heaven so much as half a day."

In conclusion, it is an infallible certainty that those who desire to be saved by Christ must endure the loss of all their works and virtues in the cause of their justification. If this doctrine is so certain, then it teaches us to be settled in the following points.

---

1. Augustine (354–430) is one of the most important theologians in the history of the church. He was the bishop of Hippo Regius in North Africa. His many important works include *The City of God* and *Confessions*.

2. Anselm (1033–1109) held the office of Archbishop of Canterbury (1093–1109). He is considered by many to be one of the most significant theologians from the time of Augustine to Aquinas. One of his most important works is *Cur Deus Homo* (Why a God-man?).

First, the Church of Rome errs grievously because it magnifies the merit of works. In so doing, it destroys the very foundation of true religion. Because they make works to be their gain in the matter of salvation, they necessarily make Christ to be their loss. Paul, on the other hand, makes all his works to be loss, so that Christ may be gain.

Second, since all virtues and works of grace are but loss for Christ, we must at conversion and throughout our lives, rest on the mercy of God and apprehend Christ alone, apart from any virtues or works in us. Nothing can satisfy the severe judgment of God except Christ. If we presume to submit any of our good works to the sentence of the law, we are sure to suffer eternal loss.

CHAPTER 4

Grace Is Freely Given

*Yet indeed I also count all things loss for the excellence
of the knowledge of Christ Jesus my Lord, for whom I
have suffered the loss of all things, and count them as
rubbish, that I may gain Christ.*
—Philippians 3:8

In the previous chapter, we observed that Paul employs
a gradation to explain how all things are loss to him: "I
also count all things loss…I have suffered the loss of all
things, and count them as rubbish." It was noted that his
use of repetition points to the certainty and the necessity
of his loss. We have considered its certainty; now follows
its necessity.

For Paul, the loss of "all things" is a necessity
because they have no part in Christ. The merit of our
virtues and works cannot stand together with the grace
of God in Christ. They are as contrary as fire and water,
and one necessarily overthrows the other in the cause
of justification and salvation. To make this clear, Paul

says that if election is "by grace, then it is no longer of works; otherwise grace is no longer grace. But if it is of works, it is no longer grace" (Rom. 11:6). Elsewhere, he writes, "You have become estranged from Christ, you who attempt to be justified by law; you have fallen from grace" (Gal. 5:4). Ambrose[1] says, "Grace is wholly received or wholly lost." To the same purpose, Augustine writes, "It is not grace if it is not freely given in every way."

There is no doubt that the Church of Rome abolishes Christ by maintaining and magnifying the merit of good works. It teaches that people are saved by their prayers, fasts, alms, pilgrimages, etc. We might well ask them: What purpose does the suffering of Christ serve? They answer that it frees us from death, gives our works the merit of eternal life, and makes them meritorious to increase our justification. But if that is true, then it means that Christ is nothing more than the first cause of our salvation, and that we are secondary causes with Him. The unavoidable implication is that Christ is not our Savior, for He is either a full and perfect Savior in Himself or He is no Savior at all.

Surely, whoever will be saved by the merit of Christ must come to Him without any virtues or works of

---

1. Ambrose (339–397) was a theologian who served as bishop of Milan (374–397). He was one of the most influential church figures of the fourth century.

their own. We must not carry the least confidence in our hearts, but esteem ourselves to be wretched and miserable sinners, and simply pray as the publican, "God, be merciful to me a sinner!" (Luke 18:13).

CHAPTER 5

When Christ Is Our Gain

Yet indeed I also count all things loss for the excellence of the knowledge of Christ Jesus my Lord, for whom I have suffered the loss of all things, and count them as rubbish, that I may gain Christ.
—Philippians 3:8

Having considered Paul's loss, we now come to the second part of his comparison: his gain. Christ is the believer's gain because, as our Mediator (God and man), He is the only fountain of all good things, whether spiritual or temporal. John says, "Of His fullness we have all received, and grace for grace" (John 1:16). Paul proclaims, "In [Him] are hidden all the treasures of wisdom and knowledge" (Col. 2:3). As Adam is the root of all evil in humanity, so Christ is the root of all grace and goodness (Rom. 5:15–19).

When does Christ become our gain? The answer is when we turn from our evil ways and believe in Him. At that very moment, He becomes our gain because He has secured many benefits for us.

The first is the forgiveness of our sins, whether past, present, or future. We must remember that pardon of sin is not given unconditionally, but it is given upon condition of repentance.

The second is the imputation of Christ's obedience in fulfilling the law for our justification before God. Whereas the first benefit brings freedom from hell and the curse of the law, this benefit brings the right to eternal life.

The third is our adoption whereby we are God's children and Christ's brothers (Rom. 8:17). Hence, we have a right of dominion over the whole creation and all things in it, whether in heaven or earth. Adam lost this right when he fell in the garden, but it is now restored in Christ. Indeed, wicked people own and use the things of this life, and they do so by God's permission. He permits them to derive some benefit from the creation to preserve their lives, but they have no right to them.

The fourth is the ministry of angels. "Are they not all ministering spirits sent forth to minister for those who will inherit salvation?" (Heb. 1:14).

The fifth is that all the miseries and calamities of this life cease to be curses, and they are turned to the good of those who are saved by Christ. "And we know that all things work together for good to those who love God, to those who are the called according to His purpose" (Rom. 8:28).

The sixth is the mortification of sin with all its parts by the virtue of Christ's death. "Knowing this, that our old man was crucified with Him, that the body of sin might be done away with, that we should no longer be slaves of sin" (Rom. 6:6).

The seventh is a spiritual life whereby we no longer live but Christ lives in us (Gal. 2:20). He makes us partakers of His anointing, thereby enabling us to live as prophets, priests, and kings. We are prophets, to teach and confess our faith in Christ. We are priests, to present our bodies and souls to God for the service of His majesty. And we are kings, to exercise rule and dominion over the lusts and corruptions of our hearts.

The eighth is that Christ presents all our prayers and good works to His Father in His own name, and thus by His own intercession He makes them acceptable to Him. "Therefore He is also able to save to the uttermost those who come to God through Him, since He always lives to make intercession for them" (Heb. 7:25).

The ninth is the presence of the Holy Spirit. When Christ ascended, He took with Him our deposit— namely our humanity, and He left His own deposit with us, the presence of the Holy Spirit to guide, comfort, and assure us of our adoption and salvation. "It is to your advantage that I go away; for if I do not go away, the Helper will not come to you; but if I depart, I will send Him to you" (John 16:7).

The tenth is perseverance in holding all these benefits.

God says, "And I will make an everlasting covenant with them, that I will not turn away from doing them good; but I will put My fear in their hearts so that they will not depart from Me" (Jer. 32:40). We must remember that these words are not only spoken generally to the church, but particularly to every member of the church, because they are the words of the covenant. David says that the righteous man is "like a tree planted by the rivers of water, that brings forth its fruit in its season, whose leaf also shall not wither" (Ps. 1:3). He always has the sap of grace in his heart.

These are the principal benefits that belong to us in Christ, thereby making Him great gain in this life.

In addition, Christ is gain when we die. This is so because He has taken away the sting of death (1 Cor. 15:55–57), and He has changed the condition of death whereby it is no longer the gate to hell but the way to eternal life. Our first gain is the resurrection of our bodies to eternal life on the day of judgment. Our second gain is the privilege of judging the world (1 Cor. 6:2). Once judgment has passed upon the godly, we will be taken up to Christ, and there, as witnesses and approvers of His sentence of condemnation, we will judge together with Him the wicked world. Our third gain is the eternal reward, according to which God will be "all in all" (1 Cor. 15:28), first in Christ and then in all the members of Christ.

And this will be our eternal gain.

CHAPTER 6

How Christ Is Our Gain

Yet indeed I also count all things loss for the excellence of the knowledge of Christ Jesus my Lord, for whom I have suffered the loss of all things, and count them as rubbish, that I may gain Christ.
—Philippians 3:8

In the previous chapter, we observed that Christ is our gain in both life and death. The next point to be handled is how Christ is our gain. According to which of His natures? We follow the ancient and orthodox doctrine that the whole Christ is our gain according to both natures. The Godhead of Christ does not profit the sinner without His manhood, nor does His manhood profit without His Godhead. Each nature works that which is proper to it, having communication with the other.

God may be considered in two ways. First, He may be considered as absolute God—that is, God absolutely considered without respect to Christ. As such, He is indeed a fountain of righteousness and life, but this fountain is closed and sealed, and not accessible to us because our sins make a separation between Him and us. God absolutely considered is a majesty full of terror to all sinful people. Second, He may be considered as God and man. He was made man, and He was manifested in our flesh (John 1:14). This, too, is a fountain of goodness. Indeed, it is the same fountain, but now opened and unsealed, flowing forth to all people. It is for this reason that Christ is called "the light of the world" (John 8:12), "the bread of life" (John 6:35), "the way, the truth, and the life" (John 14:6).

We must always remember to make a distinction between the natures of Christ. The Godhead of Christ is our gain, not in respect of essence, but in respect of virtue in and operation upon the manhood of Christ, whereby it makes all that was done and suffered in His manhood to be sufficient to appease God's anger and merit eternal life for us. As for His manhood, it is not only in effect and operation, but also really communicated to the faith of the believing heart. It is, therefore, a treasure and storehouse of all the rich graces of God, which serve to save and enrich His people of all ages throughout the whole world. If anyone doubts this, let them consider three things concerning Christ's humanity.

The first is the grace of the personal union whereby Christ's humanity is received into the unity of the second person. Christ's humanity (body and soul) has no being but in the subsistence of the second person of the

Trinity. Hence, it is truly termed the humanity of the Son of God or of the Word of God.

The second is that Christ's humanity has all fullness of grace in it (John 3:34). This fullness of grace contains all the gifts of the Holy Spirit in the highest degree of perfection. Therefore, it has more gifts for number and greater gifts for measure than all humans and angels have.

The third is that Christ's humanity receives this excellence of gifts and graces, not for itself, but that it may be a pipe or conduit to convey the same graces to all God's people. Our salvation and life depend on the fullness of the Godhead which is in Christ (Col. 2:9). But it is only conveyed to us in and by the humanity of Christ. Christ says as much when He declares, "Most assuredly, I say to you, unless you eat the flesh of the Son of Man and drink His blood, you have no life in you. Whoever eats My flesh and drinks My blood has eternal life, and I will raise him up at the last day. For My flesh is food indeed, and My blood is drink indeed. He who eats My flesh and drinks My blood abides in Me, and I in him" (John 6:53–56). John the Baptist says, "Of His fulness we have all received, and grace for grace" (John 1:16). The Lord's Supper is ordained for the increase and continuance of grace and life. Paul says of it, "The cup of blessing which we bless, is it not the communion of the blood of Christ? The bread which we break, is it not the communion of the body of Christ?" (1 Cor. 10:16).

In this manner Christ is said to have become "for us wisdom from God—and righteousness and sanctification and redemption" (1 Cor. 1:30).

First, He is our wisdom, not because the essential wisdom of the Godhead is given to us, for it is infinite and incommunicable; not because He is the author of our wisdom, giving us knowledge of our salvation as the Father and Holy Spirit do; not because He is the matter of our wisdom, the knowledge of whom is eternal life; but for a higher cause than all these. Our Mediator, the man Jesus Christ, who is also God, is a head unto us and a root of our wisdom. He was anointed with the Spirit of wisdom in His assumed manhood, not privately for Himself, but that we who believe might be partakers of the same anointing, and that wisdom from Him by His humanity might be conveyed to us. Therefore, wisdom is derived in some measure from His wisdom to all who are mystically united to Him, as light in one candle is derived to a hundred candles.

Second, Christ is our righteousness, not because His essential righteousness is given to us, for then we would all be deified. He is our righteousness, not only because He is the author and giver of our righteousness with the Father and the Holy Spirit, but because that righteousness which is in His manhood—consisting partly in the purity of His nature and partly in the purity of His action, whereby He obeyed His Father's will and suffered all things to be suffered for us—is imputed to us and accounted to be ours.

Third, Christ is our sanctification, not because the holiness of the Godhead is communicated to us, but because He was sanctified in His manhood above all humans and angels. Our holiness is derived from His holiness and springs from it as a fruit, as the corruption in Adam's posterity is derived from the corruption of Adam. Christ says, "For their sakes I sanctify Myself, that they also may be sanctified by the truth" (John 17:19). Cyril[1] writes, "As God, Christ gives Himself the Spirit; as man, He receives it. He does this not for Himself but for us, that the grace of sanctification (first received by Him) might pass out of Him to all mankind."

Fourth, Christ is our redemption. There is a double life in the person of Christ, our Mediator. One is uncreated and essential, agreeing to Christ as He is God. This life is not given to us, except in respect of its efficacy. "For in Him we live and move and have our being" (Acts 17:28). The other is the created life of the manhood, and it is either natural or spiritual. The natural life is that with which He lived in His estate of humiliation by ordinary means as all other people do. The spiritual life is that with which He now lives in the estate of exaltation and glory. He lives this life, not only for Himself, but for

---

1. Cyril (376–444) was the patriarch of Alexandria (412–444). He wrote extensively and was an important figure in the Christological controversies, especially the Council of Ephesus in 431.

us, that we, being partakers of it, may live together with Him (Rom. 6:8). Thus, the ancient church has taught that the flesh of Christ united to the Word is made quickening flesh that it might further quicken those who are united to it with spiritual life.

The estate of Christ is twofold: humiliation from His birth to His death; and exaltation in His resurrection, ascension, and present session at the right hand of God. In the first estate He works and procures our gain. Christ, lying humbly in the manger and crucified shamefully on the cross, gained our deliverance from hell and our right to eternal life. In the second estate He communicates this gain to us, and by degrees puts us in possession of it. For this end, He now sits at the right hand of God where He intercedes for us (Rom. 8:34).

The lessons are manifold.

First, it shows us that we are poor and destitute of all spiritual good things. Christ is our gain, so that He might meet our needs and fill us with graces. Otherwise, we are empty and starved with hunger.

Second, it teaches us that people who seek for the least drop of goodness outside of Christ do so in vain. He alone is the storehouse of all good things. Heaven and earth, people and angels, and all things, are as nothing to us if we seek to enjoy anything by them apart of Christ. God is not God to us without Christ.

Third, it teaches us to detest the treasury which the Church of Rome maintains and magnifies. It is a chest that contains, not only the overflow of Christ's merits, but also the merits of martyrs and saints. They are dispensed to pardon sins at the pope's pleasure. But Christ alone is our full and perfect gain, and therefore there is an all-sufficient treasury in Him. As Paul says, "you are complete in Him" (Col. 2:10). As for the merits of martyrs and saints, they bring no advantage to the people of God, but are indeed matter for the rubbish dump.

Fourth, it shows us that if Christ is our treasure and gain, our hearts must be set on Him. Our minds are usually set upon earthly gain, and we hunger after it. Let us, therefore, hunger after Christ. He alone is our gain. We must love Him and rejoice in Him above all pleasures, honors, and profits. We should be swallowed up with love for Him.

Fifth, it provides great comfort. In the loss of goods and friends, and in the face of all the calamities of this life, we are not dismayed. All the losses of this life are but small so long as we have Christ for our gain. We lack nothing amid all the losses and miseries of this world so long as we receive of the fullness of Him who is the ever-flowing fountain of goodness.

CHAPTER 7

A Desire to Know Christ

*Yet indeed I also count all things loss for the excellence
of the knowledge of Christ Jesus my Lord, for whom I
have suffered the loss of all things, and count them as
rubbish, that I may gain Christ.*
—Philippians 3:8

As already mentioned, Paul amplifies the second part
of his comparison (Christ is his gain) by using a gradation. He esteems "the excellence of the knowledge of
Christ Jesus" (v. 8); he desires to "gain Christ" (v. 8); and
he desires to "be found in Him" (v. 9). In this chapter we
will consider the first of these three degrees.

By "the knowledge of Christ Jesus," Paul means the
doctrine of the gospel or the doctrine of the person and
offices of Christ. He ascribes an excellence to this knowledge, which appears in its contents and in its effects.

The knowledge of Christ is full of excellent mysteries,
which Paul reduces to six points in 1 Timothy 3:16, "And
without controversy great is the mystery of godliness:

God was manifested in the flesh, justified in the Spirit, seen by angels, preached among the Gentiles, believed on in the world, received up in glory."

The first is the incarnation of the Son of God. "God was manifested in the flesh." Here are two wonders. First, Adam's nature and sin are inseparably joined, yet the Son of God took to Himself human nature without sin because He was conceived of a virgin by the operation of the Holy Spirit (Luke 1:35). If He had been conceived by natural generation, He would have assumed Adam's sin and corruption along with his human nature. Second, the human nature is united to the person of the Son of God, and therefore it has its subsistence by Him. It has no subsistence of its own.

The second mystery is that Christ was "justified in the Spirit." How? Christ became our surety, and He was subject to the law for us. God imputed our sins to Him and laid upon Him the punishment we deserved—that is, the first death as well as the pains of the second death. After this, Christ raised Himself from death by the power of the Godhead (by the Holy Spirit), and thereby acquitted Himself of our sins. This acquittal (or absolution) is His justification whereby He declares Himself to be a perfectly righteous Savior. If He had not satisfied the wrath of God to the full and secured perfect righteousness, He would never have risen from the dead.

The third mystery is that Christ was "seen by angels." They desired to inquire into His incarnation (1 Peter

1:12). They saw that the incarnation was a means to glorify "God in the highest," bring "on earth peace," and reveal God's "goodwill toward men" (Luke 2:14).

The fourth mystery is that Christ was "preached among the Gentiles." This is a great mystery because the knowledge of Christ was kept secret from the nations for more than four thousand years (Rom. 16:25). From the creation to Moses, the church of God was limited to a little family. From Moses to Christ, it was limited to a small nation.

The fifth mystery is that Christ was "believed on in the world." This is such a great wonder because this conversion was accomplished through the preaching of the gospel, which is flat against the natural reason and will of man, and therefore unable to persuade anyone. The preachers of the gospel were simple and silly men in the eyes of the world. Some of those who were converted were the very Jews who crucified Christ.

The sixth mystery is that Christ was "received up in glory." The greatness of this mystery appears in two things: (1) Christ's ascension was a real and full opening of the kingdom of heaven, which had formerly been shut by our sins; (2) Christ's ascension was not private, for He ascended on behalf of all God's people. They ascended in Him and with Him, and they are now in Him and with Him in glory.

Thus, we see the excellence of the knowledge of Christ in respect of its mysteries. We also learn the following.

First, if the knowledge of Christ is so excellent, then
we should not be surprised that by the devil's malice it
has been corrupted for many hundreds of years in the
Church of Rome. It teaches that the gospel is nothing
else but the law of Moses perfected. If they are right,
then Christ died in vain, and the promise of eternal life
in Christ is of no effect, and we can place our hope in
our own righteousness. The law never justifies before
God until it is perfectly kept. If men can perform this
condition of perfection, then there is no need for Christ
or the gospel.

Second, if the knowledge of Christ is of such excellence, then it must be learned in a special manner. If we
give our understanding and memory to lesser things,
then surely, we ought to apply our whole person to the
knowledge of Christ. The mind must learn it by opening
itself to conceive it. The memory must learn it by storing
it up. The will and affections must learn it by submitting
and conforming themselves to it. Thus, Paul teaches that
to learn Christ, as the truth is in Him, is to put off the
old man and put on the new man, which after God is
created in righteousness and holiness (Eph. 4:21–24).

Third, we learn to prize the knowledge of Christ
above all things in the world. David desired to be a door-
keeper in the house of God (Ps. 84:10). If he were alive
today, he would be content with an office even more humble that he might enjoy the clear light of the knowledge of
Christ. It is the fault of our times that this knowledge is

of so little value among us, and that we see so little fruit of it. It is to be feared that, because it is so little loved, God will take this treasure of knowledge from us, and send a "strong delusion" to believe lies (2 Thess. 2:11).

CHAPTER 8

A Right Knowledge

*Yet indeed I also count all things loss for the excellence
of the knowledge of Christ Jesus my Lord, for whom I
have suffered the loss of all things, and count them as
rubbish, that I may gain Christ.*
—Philippians 3:8

As noted in the previous chapter, when Paul speaks of
"the knowledge of Christ," he means the doctrine of the
person and offices of Christ. He ascribes an excellence to
this knowledge, which appears in its contents and effects.
Having considered its contents, we turn our attention to
its effects.

The first is the knowledge of God. Christ is "the
brightness of His glory and the express image of His
person" (Heb. 1:3), and He is "the image of the invisible
God" (Col. 1:15). Paul says that when God shines in our
hearts by the light of the gospel, His glory is seen "in the
face of Jesus Christ" (2 Cor. 4:6). The wisdom, power,
and goodness of God are more fully manifested in Christ

than in creation. In creation Adam (a mere man) was our head, but in the estate of grace Christ (God and man) is our Head. In creation we receive a natural life that is sustained by food, but in Christ we receive a spiritual life that is preserved eternally by the operation of the Holy Spirit. As the spouse of Adam was bone of his bone and flesh of his flesh (Gen. 2:23), so the spouse of Christ is bone of His bone and flesh of His flesh (Eph. 5:30). This is true in a more excellent manner because every person, as he is born again, arises out of the merit and efficacy of the blood that flowed from the side of Christ. In creation God makes life from nothing, but in Christ He draws our life from death and changes death itself into life. In the law the justice of God is set down and revealed, but in Christ we see God's perfect justice and mercy revealed to the full. We also see justice and mercy reconciled. In Christ we see the length, breadth, height, and depth of the love of God (Eph. 3:18–19), in that He promises to love His people with the same love with which He loves Christ (John 17:23).

The second effect is the knowledge of self. First, we must consider that in His suffering Christ took our persons upon Him, and that upon the cross He stood in our place. Second, we are to consider the greatness of His agony set forth in four things: (1) Christ's complaint that His soul was "exceedingly sorrowful, even to death" (Matt. 26:38); (2) Christ's prayer to His Father that "if it is possible, let this cup pass from Me" (Matt. 26:39);

(3) Christ's weariness that necessitated an angel from heaven to come and strengthen Him (Luke 22:43); (4) Christ's sweat that "became like great drops of blood falling down to the ground" (Luke 22:44). When we see Christ's agony, we see the greatness of God's anger against us for our sins. We see the greatness of our sins and the vileness of our persons. We see the hardness of our hearts, in that we never so much as sigh for our offences which caused the Son of God to sweat water and blood. We see our ingratitude, in that we so little regard Christ's work. We see our duty, that we are to be thoroughly touched with true repentance, and to humble ourselves (as it were) to the very pit of hell. If the Son of God cries for our sins imputed to Him, we are much more to cry and bleed in our hearts for them, seeing that they are ours and they have pierced Him (Zech. 12:10).

Paul commends this knowledge to us by calling it "the knowledge of Christ Jesus my Lord" (Phil. 3:8). He is our Lord in four ways: (1) by right of donation—in His eternal counsel the Father gives all the elect to Christ; (2) by right of creation; (3) by right of redemption; (4) by right of headship—as a living head Christ gives spiritual life (sense and motion) to all who believe in Him. Paul calls Christ his "Lord" because he knows he belongs to Him by election, creation, redemption, and spiritual conjunction with Him. Paul's example teaches us two things.

First, it teaches us how we are to know Christ and the doctrine of the gospel. A right knowledge requires a general understanding of Christ and His benefits as well as a special application of Christ and His benefits. It is not sufficient to believe the election, redemption, justification, and glorification of God's people. We must go further by believing these things to be ours. The reason is taken from the two chief parts of the gospel. The first is a promise in which Christ and all His benefits are offered to us, and the second is a commandment to apply the promise and its substance to ourselves by faith (1 John 3:23). Those who ignore this second part neglect half the gospel. Here is the foundation of the saving knowledge that justifies and brings eternal life (Isa. 53:11; John 17:3).

Second, Paul's example teaches us to subject ourselves (body and soul) to Christ. In calling Christ "Lord," Paul acknowledges that he is His servant. The end of all preaching is to bring our words, deeds, and thoughts in subjection to Christ (2 Cor. 10:5). The purpose of Christ's session in glory at the right hand of the Father is that every knee may bow to Him (Phil. 2:10–11). It behooves us, therefore, to live as true and sincere servants of Christ.

CHAPTER 9

A Desire to Win Christ

Yet indeed I also count all things loss for the excellence of the knowledge of Christ Jesus my Lord, for whom I have suffered the loss of all things, and count them as rubbish, that I may gain Christ.
—Philippians 3:8

The second degree in Paul's gradation is his desire to "gain Christ" (v. 8). By this he means he desires to make Christ his gain. This appears by the opposition of the words, for he says that he deprived himself of all things (that is, counted all things as loss) that he might win Christ.

Christ is made our gain when we do two things. First, we make Him ours—that is, we make Him our Christ (or my Christ) in particular. A twofold consent is required to make this possible. (1) God's consent that Christ will be ours. He gives His consent in the revelation of the promise touching the woman's seed, which was made to our first parents. "And I will put enmity between you and the woman, and between your seed and her Seed; He shall bruise your head, and you shall bruise His heel" (Gen. 3:15). He gives it in the continual renewing of the promise to our forefathers. "And I will establish My covenant between Me and you and your descendants after you in their generations, for an ever-lasting covenant, to be God to you and your descendants after you" (Gen. 17:7). He gives it in the incarnation and passion of Christ. "But when the fulness of the time had come, God sent forth His Son, born of a woman, born under the law, to redeem those who were under the law, that we might receive the adoption as sons" (Gal. 4:4–5). He gives it in the preaching of the gospel. "That if you confess with your mouth the Lord Jesus and believe in your heart that God has raised Him from the dead, you will be saved" (Rom. 10:9). He gives it in the administration of baptism and the Lord's Supper. "The cup of blessing which we bless, is it not the communion of the blood of Christ? The bread which we break, is it not the communion of the body of Christ?" (1 Cor. 10:16). (2) Our consent to receive Christ. We give it when we believe in Him, when we begin to be touched in our hearts for our sins and to hunger and thirst after Him. And so it is that by the concurrence of these two consents, Christ is really made ours.

Second, Christ is made our gain when we place our confidence in Him. We must fix our hearts upon Him alone for the forgiveness of our sins and the salvation of our souls. Where our gain is, there our hearts must be.

When riches increase, we must not set our hearts upon them. Though they are good things, they are not our gain or treasure. Christ is not only a good thing to us, but the very fountain of all good things. For this reason, we bestow our hearts on Him.

Our affections must be satisfied and filled with the desire of Christ until we have the full fruition of Him. Paul says, "For to me, to live is Christ, and to die is gain" (Phil. 1:21). In other words, Christ was his gain in life and death. In our text, he says that he desires to "gain Christ" (Phil. 3:8). Naturally, our desires are insatiable in respect of riches, honors, and pleasures, but we must learn to moderate ourselves in seeking these things and learn to be content with the portion that God allots us (Phil. 4:11). In addition, the insatiableness of our affections must be turned toward Christ. The woman, who had the hemorrhage, only desired to touch the hem of Christ's garment (Luke 8:43–48). We must go further. We must desire, not only to touch Him, but to lay hold on Him with both hands and hang on to Him. Thomas desired to put his finger into Christ's side (John 20:25). We must set Christ crucified before our eyes, so that we behold His precious blood (so to speak) flowing afresh from His hands, feet, and side. We must not only touch His blood, but sprinkle ourselves with it—yes, immerse ourselves in it, body, soul, and all.

CHAPTER 10

A Desire to Be
Found in Christ

*And be found in Him, not having my own righteous-
ness, which is from the law, but that which is through
faith in Christ, the righteousness which is from God
by faith.*
—Philippians 3:9

The third degree in Paul's gradation is that he desired to
be "found" in Christ. To be in Christ is to be taken out of
the first Adam and united to Christ as His very flesh or
as a true member of His spiritual body. This incorpora-
tion into Christ is a mystery. If we want to understand it,
we must observe four rules.

The first is that our whole person is united to
the whole person of Christ. The Redeemer and the
redeemed are one. Christ (God and man) redeemed us,
not only in soul but also in body. Therefore, we have
our whole persons united to the whole person of Christ.
Paul asks, "Do you not know that your bodies are members of Christ?" (1 Cor. 6:15). Christ says, "He who eats

My flesh and drinks My blood abides in Me, and I in him" (John 6:56).

The second rule touches the order of this union: we are first joined to the manhood of Christ and by His manhood to His Godhead. That which brings us into fellowship with God joins us to Him. It is by the humanity of Christ that we have fellowship with God. It is as the veil of the temple whereby the high priest entered into the holy of holies and the presence of God (Heb. 10:20). Christ's humanity serves as a pipe or conduit to derive the efficacy and operation of the Godhead to us.

The third rule is that this union is not imagined but is a true and real conjunction. Distance does not hinder this union; we are on earth and the humanity of Christ is in heaven. After the contract of marriage, two distinct persons, though a thousand miles asunder, remain one flesh. If this is true in nature, may not the same be found in this union that is above nature?

The fourth rule is that the bond of this conjunction is the Holy Spirit, who is both in Christ and us. John teaches this, saying that Christ "abides in us, by the Spirit whom He has given us" (1 John 3:24). This Spirit works faith in us, which also knits us to Christ who dwells in our hearts "through faith" (Eph. 3:17). This shows us that distance does not hinder this union. The Holy Spirit, being infinite, may dwell in Christ and us. Though our faith is seated in our hearts, it can reach forth and apprehend Christ in heaven.

Paul's desire is that he may be "found" in Christ—that is, that God would consider him to be a member of Christ and accept him into His favor for Christ. To understand this, we must give attention to the order that God uses in showing His love. He begins with His love for Christ, whom He loves simply for Himself. Then, He descends from Christ to those who are united to Christ, whereby He considers them to be a part of Christ. He loves them, not simply, but respectively in and for Christ. When we look upon different objects through a green glass, they all appear to be green. Even so, those whom God sees in Christ are loved by Him as Christ is loved, and they are righteous as He is righteous. This is how Paul desires to be found on the day of judgment.

What does this teach us?

First, we learn that God will examine our hearts, lives, and works on the day of judgment. As Paul mentions, this presupposes that God sees and observes our ways, and that He will reveal them one day. He knows even now whether we are in Christ or not. For this reason, we are to call ourselves to a strict account. God will discover what is amiss, though we might be able to hide it from others. It is upon this ground that Solomon dissuades young men from fornication. "For why should you, my son, be enraptured by an immoral woman, and be embraced in the arms of a seductress? For the ways of man are before the eyes of the LORD, and He ponders all his paths" (Prov. 5:20–21). To this purpose the Jews have a saying that is worth remembering: "Write three things in your heart, and you will never sin. There is an eye that sees you, an ear that hears you, and a hand that writes all your sayings and doings in a book." The cause of our many sins is that we falsely think that God neither sees nor hears us. Hence, David says of his enemies: "Indeed, they belch with their mouth; swords are in their lips; for they say, 'Who hears?'" (Ps. 59:7).

Second, we see that Paul's principal care, the object of all his desires, was that he might be found by God on the day of judgment to be a member of Christ. This must be our main care—to be knit to Christ and, therefore, accepted by God when we rise to judgment. Christ declares, "Watch therefore, and pray always that you may be counted worthy to escape all these things that will come to pass, and to stand before the Son of Man" (Luke 21:36). We cannot do this unless we are incorporated into Christ. We are bidden to seek first the kingdom of heaven, which means to be in Christ. To be wise in many things, yet neglect the main thing, is the greatest folly of all. What is the fault of the foolish virgins (Matt. 25:1–13)? They carried the burning lamps of a Christian profession. They had the oil of grace. But they did not have enough oil to supply their lamps. Their fault was that they did not have the foresight to furnish themselves with sufficient oil. There is never a sufficiency of oil until we are true members of Christ. Their damnable folly was that they contented themselves with a mere profession of Christ, but they did not have a special care to be members of Christ.

Let us diligently endeavor to be in this life what we desire to be before God on the day of judgment. We will undergo three judgments—the judgment of men, the judgment of ourselves, and the judgment of God. We may falsify the first two, but we cannot falsify the third. We may deceive men and ourselves, but we cannot deceive God. It is the foundation of all good things to be engrafted into Christ, and all other cares and concerns should give way to this.

Someone might ask, what must I do to be in Christ? There are two things: (1) you must break off all your sins and turn to God; (2) you must pray earnestly that your heart may be knit to Christ.

It might be asked how we may know that we are in Christ? John tells us: "By this we know that we abide in Him, and He in us, because He has given us of His Spirit" (1 John 4:13). We may know that we have the Spirit of Christ if the same mind, inclination, and disposition, the same love of God and man, the same meekness, patience, and obedience are in us which were in Christ. The same fruit argues the same Holy Spirit.

CHAPTER 11

A Double Righteousness

And be found in Him, not having my own righteous-
ness, which is from the law, but that which is through
faith in Christ, the righteousness which is from God
by faith; that I may know Him and the power of
His resurrection, and the fellowship of His sufferings,
being conformed to His death, if, by any means, I
may attain to the resurrection from the dead.
—Philippians 3:9–11

Having taught in general terms that Christ is his gain,
Paul now declares it in more particular terms. He sets
down a threefold gain which he desired to obtain from
Christ. The first is the righteousness of Christ. The
second is fellowship with Christ. The third is the resurrection of the body unto eternal life.

In this chapter we will begin our examination of the
first of these: the righteousness of Christ. It is described
in verse 9, "And be found in Him, not having my own
righteousness, which is from the law, but that which

is through faith in Christ, the righteousness which is from God by faith." These words are an explanation of what it means to "be found" in Christ. Simply put, Paul desired to be accepted by God for Christ's sake and to be esteemed righteous in Christ's righteousness.

To explain what he means, Paul describes two kinds of righteousness. The first is his "own" righteousness. It is in him, and it is exercised by the powers of his soul— namely, his mind, will, and affections. In addition, it is "of the law"—that is, of the works which the law requires. According to Paul, "the righteousness which is of the law" is that "the man who does those things shall live by them" (Rom. 10:5).

The second kind of righteousness is "through faith in Christ." It arises from the obedience of Christ, and it is apprehended by faith. The expression, "faith in Christ," refers to faith in the blood of Christ (Rom. 3:22, 25). This righteousness is not our "own," but "is from God." In other words, it is not of us in whole or in part, but God freely gives it to us when we believe.

Here Paul introduces a weighty point of doctrine— namely, there is a double righteousness: the first is of the law, and the second is of the gospel. He sees these two kinds of righteousness as opposites in the case of justification.

Regarding the righteousness of the law, Paul says that it is in us. In a word, it is a conformity of our heart and life to the will of God, as revealed in the law of God.

The law knows nothing of the righteousness that is outside of us. Paul also says that it consists of such virtues and works as the law prescribes.

Regarding the righteousness of the gospel, Paul sets it forth by emphasizing four things. First, it is not in us, but outside of us. Second, it is in Christ. "Now this is His name by which He will be called, THE LORD OUR RIGHTEOUSNESS" (Jer. 23:6). Christ must be considered in two ways: as God and as Mediator. According to these two, He has a double righteousness. As God His righteousness is infinite, and therefore incommunicable. As Mediator His righteousness is His obedience which He performed in His manhood, consisting of His suffering in life and death, and His fulfilling of the law for us. This obedience, which is in Christ and not in us, is the very matter of the righteousness of the gospel. Third, this righteousness is made ours by faith, which rests on Christ and applies His obedience to us. Fourth, the author of this righteousness is God. Out of His grace and mercy, He freely gives Christ and His obedience to us when we believe.

From these four points we derive a definition of the righteousness of the gospel. In a word, it is the righteousness of the Mediator—namely, the obedience of Christ, given to us by God and received by faith.

This shows us the difference between legal and evangelical righteousness, between the law and the gospel. The law promises life upon the condition of our works, or upon the condition of our obedience performed according to the tenor of the law. On the other hand, the gospel does not require the condition of merit, nor does it require any work on our part in the case of our justification. It only prescribes us to believe in Christ and to rest on His obedience as our righteousness before God's tribunal.

CHAPTER 12

The Obedience of Christ

And be found in Him, not having my own righteousness, which is from the law, but that which is through faith in Christ, the righteousness which is from God by faith.
—Philippians 3:9

These words explain what it means to "be found" in Christ. In sum, it is to possess a righteousness that is "through faith in Christ," meaning it arises from the obedience of Christ, and it is apprehended by faith. As discussed in the last chapter, this leads to a weighty point of doctrine—namely, there is a double righteousness: the first is of the law, and the second is of the gospel. A second point of doctrine is as follows: a sinner stands just before the tribunal seat of God, not by the righteousness of the law, but by the righteousness of faith, which is the obedience of Christ. Because this point of doctrine is so important (and doubted by many), I will confirm it with six reasons.

First, God manifests His mercy and justice to the full in the justification of sinners. Paul says that God justifies "freely by His grace" (Rom. 3:24), and in justifying He is "just and the justifier of the one who has faith in Jesus" (v. 26). This concurrence of mercy and justice is only found in the obedience of Christ, performed by Him on our behalf. As for all Christian virtues and works, God accepts them by His mercy, but they do not satisfy His justice according to the tenor of the law.

Second, Abraham, the father of all the faithful, was justified without works (Rom. 4:1–2). His faith (that is, the Messiah apprehended by his faith) "was accounted to him for righteousness" (v. 3). He is a pattern for us, meaning we must be justified as he was justified.

Third, Paul declares, "As by one man's disobedience many were made sinners, so also by one Man's obedience many will be made righteous" (Rom. 5:19). We are made sinners by Adam's disobedience imputed to us; therefore, we are made righteous by the obedience of Christ imputed to us. Bernard[1] says, "Whom another man's fault defiled, another man's water washed." In calling it another man's fault, he does not deny that it is ours. It is ours because we have sinned in Adam, and God has imputed it to us by His just judgment. Yet, mercifully,

---

1. Bernard of Clairvaux (1090–1153) was cofounder of the Knights Templars and the founder of Clairvaux Abbey. Perhaps his best known literary works are *On Loving God* and *Sermons on the Song of Songs*.

God gives us the obedience of Christ. Bernard clearly teaches the doctrine of imputed righteousness, saying, "All are dead that the satisfaction of one might be imputed to all, as He alone bore the sins of all." He adds, "Death is put to flight by the death of Christ, and the righteousness of Christ is imputed to us."

Fourth, we are "in Christ Jesus, who became for us wisdom from God—and righteousness" (1 Cor. 1:30)—that is, righteousness imputed. In the next words, he says that Christ is made unto us "sanctification"—that is, inherent righteousness.

Fifth, as Christ was made sin, so we are made the righteousness of God. Christ was made sin not by conveying any corruption into Him, but by imputation. Similarly, we are made the righteousness of God by imputation. In case anyone should think that this righteousness is not imputed to us, but infused into us, Paul says that we have "become the righteousness of God in Him"—that is, in Christ (2 Cor. 5:21). It follows, therefore, that there is no virtue or work in us that justifies before God, and that our righteousness, whereby we are just in God's sight and accepted to eternal life, is outside of us and found in Christ. Christ was made sin that we might be made righteous, not our righteousness but God's righteousness, not in us but in Him.

Sixth, before the fall, man was under obligation to fulfill the law. This debt was to be paid daily to God. After the fall, man doubled his debt. He still owes the debt of fulfilling the law, and he now owes to God a satisfaction due for breaking the law. Our nonpayment of this twofold debt is our unrighteousness. Where can we find a sufficient payment for this debt? We daily increase our debt by our many sins. Our own works, though proceeding from faith, are not a satisfactory payment because we cannot pay one debt by another. And if we search through heaven and earth, we will find nothing to stand as a payment to God except the obedience of the Redeemer. He has presented His obedience before the throne of the Almighty as an endless treasure to make payment for us. Because His obedience is a satisfaction for our unrighteousness, it is also our righteousness in the acceptance of God.

By these reasons it appears that the only thing that can absolve us before God, and procure the right to eternal life, is the obedience of the Mediator (God and man), without any virtues or works on our part.

Some people corrupt the article of justification by mingling things which can no more be combined than fire and water—namely, the righteousness of the gospel and the righteousness of the law. The Church of Rome makes a double justification. The first contains two parts: the pardon of sin by the death of Christ, and the infused habit of charity. The second is by works, which (they say) meritoriously increase the first justification and procure eternal life. Here we see the sovereign medicine of the gospel (namely, the remission of sins) tempered with the poison of the law. Virtues and works have their place as God's good gifts in our lives. But when they are brought within the circle of justification as meritorious causes, they are out of place and are no better than poison. It is for this reason that Paul calls them "loss" and "rubbish."

But many object, claiming that the obedience of Christ (that is, the righteousness of another) cannot possibly be our righteousness.

My answer is that the righteousness of another may be ours if it is really made ours. And this is true in Christ. When we believe in Him, though our persons remain distinct, we are made one with Him. According to the tenor of the evangelical covenant, we are given to Him, and He is given to us, so that we may truly say "Christ is mine." If Christ is ours, then His obedience is not only His but ours. It is His because it is in Him. It is ours because God gives it to us when He gives Christ to us.

Many claim that when Paul rejects the righteousness of the law, he means the works of the law which are performed by the strength of nature, but not the works of grace.

My answer is that Paul is speaking of himself in the present as he is a Christian and apostle. Therefore, he excludes his own righteousness, even as an apostle. "What shall we say then? Shall we continue in sin that grace may abound?" (Rom. 6:1). This objection cannot be inferred from the notion of justification by works of grace. The objection only arises from the doctrine of justification by the obedience of Christ imputed to us without any of our own works.

We are justified, not by the righteousness of the law, but by the righteousness of faith. Here is the foundation of our comfort. If we are tempted in this life, we must appeal to this righteousness against the tempter. If Satan pleads against us that we are sinners, and therefore subject to eternal damnation, let us answer him by proclaiming that the obedience of Christ has freed us from damnation. If he pleads that we never fulfilled the law and, consequently, we have no right to eternal life, we must answer him by proclaiming that Christ fulfilled the law for us. If he vexes us with our many wants and corruptions, let us tell him that so long as we turn to God from all our evil ways, bewail our corruptions, and believe in Christ, all our wants are covered in His obedience. If, in the time of death, the fear of God's judgment terrifies us, we are to uphold our Mediator's obedience and place it between God's anger and us. We are to rest upon it and wrap our souls in it. The prophet Isaiah says that the Messiah is "a hiding place (shelter) from the wind (burning heat of the wrath of God)" (Isa. 32:2). Paul says that Christ is "a propitiation" (Rom. 3:25). As the mercy seat covered the ark and the law that was in the ark from the presence of God, so Christ covers our sins and puts Himself between us and God's indignation.

CHAPTER 13

The Gift of Faith

*And be found in Him, not having my own righteous-
ness, which is from the law, but that which is through
faith in Christ, the righteousness which is from God
by faith.*

—Philippians 3:9

Here Paul explains that to "be found" in Christ is to
possess a righteousness that is "through faith in Christ,"
meaning it arises from the obedience of Christ, and it is
apprehended by faith. To this point, we have considered
two doctrines which emerge from this verse. First, there
is a double righteousness: one is of the law, and one is of
the gospel. Second, a sinner stands just before the tribunal seat of God, not by the righteousness of the law, but
by the righteousness of faith, which is the obedience of
Christ. We now turn our attention to a third doctrine:
faith is the means to receive and obtain the obedience of
Christ for our righteousness.

What is faith? It is a special gift of God whereby

we believe Christ and His benefits to be ours. It is a gift of God because it comes wholly from Him and not from our mind or will. Paul says, "For to you it has been granted on the behalf of Christ, not only to believe in Him, but also to suffer for His sake" (Phil. 1:29). Christ our Savior says to two of His disciples: "O foolish ones, and slow of heart to believe" (Luke 24:25). Some might object that when we first believe, we do so willingly. I say it is indeed so. But this willingness is not in us by nature, but by grace. When God gives us the gift of faith, He gives us the will to believe. "No one can come to Me unless the Father who sent Me draws him; and I will raise him up at the last day" (John 6:44). To be drawn to Christ is to have our will changed, whereby we are made willing by God's power.

There are two reasons why faith in Christ is a special gift. First, it is not only above corrupt human nature, but above Adam's created and incorrupt human nature before the fall. Faith was never in human nature by creation. Adam never had it, nor did the moral law reveal it to him. Other virtues (such as the love of God and the fear of God) are revealed by the law, and they were in human nature by creation. While all other gifts of God are given to those who are ingrafted into Christ, faith is given to those who are to be ingrafted. Faith is the ingrafting, and therefore it is not given to those who are already in Christ but to those who are about to be in Christ.

Furthermore, I say that faith is believing that

Christ and His benefits are ours. This is the property of faith whereby it differs from all the other graces of God. When Thomas had put his finger into Christ's side, he said, "My Lord and my God!" Christ replied, "Thomas, because you have seen Me, you have believed. Blessed are those who have not seen and yet have believed" (John 20:28–29). Here we see that faith is to believe that Christ is our Lord and our God. Paul says, "I live by faith in the Son of God." He shows what he means by faith in the very next words: "who loved me and gave Himself for me" (Gal. 2:20). There are two main reasons why I say that faith is believing that Christ is our Christ.

The first is God's command to believe that Christ and His benefits are ours. "And this is His commandment: that we should believe on the name of His Son Jesus Christ and love one another, as He gave us commandment" (1 John 3:23). To believe in Christ is to put our confidence in Him. We cannot put our confidence in Him unless we are first assured that He and His benefits are ours. He tells us, "Whatever things you ask when you pray, believe that you receive them, and you will have them" (Mark 11:24). Above all things we are to ask that God may give us Christ and His benefits. To ask it, we must believe it.

The second reason is the way God offers the promise of grace to us. He does not only announce it to us generally but applies it to us personally. How? First, God confirms it by an oath, so that we might apply it and derive comfort from it. "That by two immutable things, in which it is impossible for God to lie, we might have strong consolation, who have fled for refuge to lay hold of the hope set before us" (Heb. 6:18). Second, God gives us the Spirit of adoption, who bears witness to our conscience of those things that God has given to us. These things are only offered generally in the promise but applied particularly by the Holy Spirit. Paul says, "The Spirit Himself bears witness with our spirit that we are children of God" (Rom. 8:16). This testimony must be certain, and it must be known by us, otherwise it is not a true testimony. Third, both the sacraments are seals of the promise. In these God offers Christ to us, and He writes our names within the promise, so that we might not doubt.

As God gives the promise, so we must receive it by faith. God gives it and applies it; therefore, we must receive it and by faith apply it to ourselves. If anyone says that he cannot conceive his faith upon these two grounds, I say that he must strive against his unbelief and endeavor to believe by desiring, asking, seeking, and knocking. God will accept the will to believe for faith itself, so long as there is an honest heart touched with sorrow for past sins and a purpose to sin no more.

There are two kinds of false faith. The first is when a person conceives in his heart a strong persuasion that Christ is his Savior, yet he carries in his heart a resolve to sin and makes no change in his life. His persuasion is nothing but presumption. It is a counterfeit faith, for an essential property of true faith is a desire to purify the heart and to show itself in prayer and repentance.

The second kind of false faith is when a man conceives a strong persuasion that Christ is his Savior, yet he despises the ministry of the Word and sacraments. This is another counterfeit faith, for true faith is conceived and confirmed by the Word and sacraments. We must look for Christ where God offers Him to us. In the Word and sacraments, He opens His hand and sets forth all the blessings of Christ to us. We must not imagine that we can find Christ wherever we like, but we must seek Him in the Word and sacraments. We must receive Him there if we desire to receive Him correctly.

We must prove whether we have faith or not, because where there is no faith, there is no righteousness. Our duty is to labor for such a faith that can justify itself to be true faith by works of love to God and others. By faith we must rest wholly on Christ's obedience in life and death. Though God should reach out His hand and destroy us, we must still rest upon Him.

CHAPTER 14

Faith Alone

And be found in Him, not having my own righteousness, which is from the law, but that which is through faith in Christ, the righteousness which is from God by faith.

—Philippians 3:9

Faith is the means to receive and obtain the obedience of Christ for our righteousness. But how exactly is faith a means to obtain righteousness? Faith does not justify as a work of God in us. If it did, then all graces (love, hope, patience, etc.) would be a means of justification. Nor does it justify as an excellent virtue, for it is imperfect and mingled with unbelief. Nor does it justify as a means of preparing us for justification, for as soon as we begin to believe in Christ, we are justified without any preparation coming between faith and justification. Nor does it justify because it contains other virtues and works, as the kernel contains the tree with all its branches, for then it would be the principal part of our righteousness. Paul distinguishes between righteousness and faith, saying that our righteousness is of God "through faith" (Rom. 3:22). It is "through faith," not "for faith."

Faith is the means to obtain righteousness because it is an instrument by which we receive the benefits of Christ as ours. This apprehension is made when we indeed believe that Christ and His benefits are ours. Some people might think that it is the very act of faith in apprehending Christ that justifies. But we must understand that faith does not apprehend by a power from itself but by virtue of the covenant. If a person believes that the kingdom of France is his, this does not make it his. But if he believes that Christ and His kingdom are His, it is indeed His, not because he simply believes but because he believes upon God's command and promise. In the covenant, God promises to impute Christ's obedience to us for our righteousness if we believe.

Is faith helped by other virtues? No. Faith alone is the means to obtain the righteousness of Christ. It does so without the help of any other virtue or work. Paul teaches that faith apprehends Christ for righteousness "without the law"—that is, without anything that the law requires from us. This teaches us three things. The first is that nothing in us is an efficient or meritorious cause, in whole or in part, of our justification or reconciliation with God. The second is that nothing but faith is ordained by God to be a hand to receive His favor in the merit of Christ. The third is that our sanctification is not a part of our justification, which stands wholly in the imputation of the righteousness of Christ. In a word, Paul excludes all things that are in us, whether by nature or grace, from the act of justification.

Someone might object that Abraham was not justified by faith alone, but by works. "Was not Abraham our father justified by works when he offered Isaac his son on the altar?" (James 2:21). The answer is that there is a double justification. The first is the justification of the person, whereby a sinner is made no sinner. The second is the justification of the faith of the person, whereby faith is declared to be true faith. This second justification is by works. "But someone will say, 'You have faith, and I have works.' Show me your faith without your works, and I will show you my faith by my works" (v. 18). When James says that Abraham was "justified by works," he means that by his works he justified himself to be a true believer, even the father of all the faithful. By works his "faith was made perfect"—that is, declared to be a true faith (v. 22).

Is faith always alone? It is alone at the beginning of our conversion, and in our salvation's continuance and final accomplishment. Paul desires to stand before God on the day of judgment by the righteousness of faith without his own righteousness of the law (Phil. 3:9). He introduces Abraham as one who was justified by his faith in Christ (Rom. 4:2–3). He says three things about faith: (1) by it "we have access" into God's grace; (2) by it we "stand" in the same grace; (3) by it we "rejoice in hope of the glory of God" (Rom. 5:2).

By all that has been said, we see how righteousness comes by faith in Christ. If our righteousness is outside of us, and we must trust God for it, then we must also trust Him for health, wealth, liberty, peace, food, clothing, and for all the things of this life. If we cannot trust Him in the lesser, we will never trust Him in the greater. Therefore, we are to walk in the duties of our callings and obey God in them. We must trust Him for the success of our labors. When all worldly helps fail, we must still trust Him. If we cannot trust Him for our temporal life, we will never trust Him for our salvation.

In conclusion, there is only one way of justification—namely, we are justified and accepted by God to eternal life by grace alone through faith alone in Christ alone. It is faith alone in the beginning, middle, and end of our salvation.

CHAPTER 15

Christ's Resurrection

*And be found in Him, not having my own righteous-
ness, which is from the law, but that which is through
faith in Christ, the righteousness which is from God
by faith; that I may know Him and the power of
His resurrection, and the fellowship of His sufferings,
being conformed to His death, if, by any means, I
may attain to the resurrection from the dead.*
—Philippians 3:9–11

Here Paul mentions a threefold gain which he desired
to obtain from Christ. The first is the righteousness of
Christ. The second is fellowship with Christ. The third
is the resurrection of the body unto eternal life.

We have considered the first; now we turn our
attention to the second. Paul sets it forth generally: "that
I may know Him." It must be remembered that knowledge is twofold: knowledge by faith and knowledge by
experience. The first is to be assured of Christ and His
benefits, though it is against all human reason, hope,

and experience. "And this is eternal life, that they may know You, the only true God, and Jesus Christ whom You have sent" (John 17:3). The second is to have a sense and feeling of our inward fellowship with Christ, and by observing His goodness to grow more and more in the experience of His love. It is this knowledge that Paul intends in our text. His desire is that he may grow more and more in the holy experience of the endless love of God and fellowship with Christ.

There are two parts to this fellowship: fellowship with Christ in His resurrection, and fellowship with Christ in His death. Paul desires to "know Him and the power of His resurrection." What is Christ's resurrection? A right understanding of it rests on five truths.

The first concerns the person of Christ. He arose as God and man. Indeed, it was only His body that arose from the grave, and not His soul or His Godhead. But by reason of the union of the two natures in the one person, the whole Christ (God and man) arose. This commends to us the excellence of Christ's resurrection and makes it the foundation of our resurrection.

The second point concerns the people for whom Christ arose. He did not arise as a private person, but He arose for us—that is, in our place. When He arose, all His people arose with Him and in Him. Paul says that God "raised us up together, and made us sit together in the heavenly places in Christ Jesus" (Eph. 2:6). His resurrection, therefore, was public. And it is the ground of our comfort.

The third point concerns when Christ arose. He did so when He lay in bondage under death in the grave. God raised Christ, "having loosed the pains of death, because it was not possible that He should be held by it" (Acts 2:24). When Peter says that God "loosed the pains of death," he means that Christ was made captive for a time to the first death and to the sorrow of the second death. But He raised Himself from this captivity and bondage, which means that His resurrection is a full victory over death and all our spiritual enemies.

The fourth point concerns how Christ arose. It was by His own power. "Therefore My Father loves Me, because I lay down My life that I may take it again. No one takes it from Me, but I lay it down of Myself. I have power to lay it down, and I have power to take it again. This command I have received from My Father" (John 10:17–18). If this had not been the case, even if He had arisen a thousand times by the power of another, He would not have been a perfect Redeemer.

The fifth point concerns the nature of Christ's resurrection. It consists of three actions. The first is the reuniting of His body and His soul, which had been severed for a time, though neither of them was ever severed from the Godhead. The second action is the changing of His natural life, which He had in the estate of humiliation, into a heavenly and spiritual life without infirmities

(1 Cor. 15:52–55). It was no longer maintained by food. After His resurrection, He never ate food out of necessity, but upon one occasion to manifest the truth of His manhood. Christ took this heavenly and spiritual life to Himself that He might convey it to all who believe in Him. The third action is His emerging from the grave whereby death itself acknowledged Him to be a conqueror, and that it had no claim over Him.

CHAPTER 16

The Power of Christ's Resurrection

That I may know Him and the power of His res-
urrection, and the fellowship of His sufferings, being
conformed to His death.
                                            —Philippians 3:10

Having considered the nature of Christ's resurrection in the last chapter, we come now to consider its power. In brief, it is the power of His Godhead or the power of His Spirit, whereby He raised Himself from death to life on our behalf. Its excellence may be known by its effects.

First, by His resurrection Christ demonstrates that He is the true and perfect Savior of the world. It was foretold that the Messiah would die and rise again. "For You will not leave my soul in Sheol, nor will You allow Your Holy One to see corruption" (Ps. 16:10). "For as Jonah was three days and three nights in the belly of the great fish, so will the Son of Man be three days and three nights in the heart of the earth" (Matt. 12:40). All this was accomplished by the power of Christ's resurrection.

Second, by His resurrection Christ shows that He is the true and natural Son of God. He was "declared to be the Son of God with power according to the Spirit of holiness, by the resurrection from the dead" (Rom. 1:4).

Third, by His resurrection Christ declares that He had made a full and perfect satisfaction for the sins of the world. If He had not satisfied to the full, He would not have risen from the dead. Paul says, "If Christ is not risen, your faith is futile; you are still in your sins!" (1 Cor. 15:17). Because He is risen, the opposite is true—those who believe in Him are no longer in their sins. "Who is he who condemns? It is Christ who died, and further-more is also risen, who is even at the right hand of God, who also makes intercession for us" (Rom. 8:34).

Fourth, by His resurrection Christ secures our jus-tification. Paul testifies that Christ "was delivered up because of our offenses, and was raised because of our justification" (Rom. 4:25). When He was on the cross, He was there in our place, having our sins imputed to Him. When He arose from the dead, He acquitted and justified Himself from our sins, and He ceased to be a reputed sinner for us. Therefore, all those who believe in Him are acquitted, absolved, and justified in Him from all their sins. What about those who lived in the times of the Old Testament, before Christ's resurrection? How could they be justified, seeing as the effect must follow the cause? The answer is that they were justified by the future resurrection of Christ. Though it followed in time, its value and virtue reach back to the beginning of the world.

Fifth, by His resurrection Christ bestows all the gifts and graces which He merited and procured for us by His death. Thus, He testifies that the giving of the Holy Spirit in fullness was reserved for His glorification (John 7:39), which began at His resurrection. Peter says that God's people are "begotten…to a living hope through the resurrection of Jesus Christ from the dead" (1 Peter 1:3). By reason of this bestowal of graces and gifts, Christ's resurrection is the beginning of a new and spiritual world which the Holy Spirit calls "the world to come" (Heb. 2:5). There will be new heavens and a new earth (Isa. 65:17). This one effect sufficiently declares the excellence of the power of Christ's resurrection.

Sixth, by His resurrection Christ raises us from the death of sin to newness of life. The reason is plain. In His resurrection Christ puts away His natural life, which He received along with our nature from Adam, and He took to Himself a spiritual life, that He might communicate it to all who believe in Him. As the first Adam makes us like him in sin and death, so the last Adam (Christ) renews us and makes us like Him in righteousness and life (Rom. 5:18–19). Quickened with spiritual life, the Head will not allow the members to remain in the death of sin.

Seventh, by His resurrection Christ preserves safe-and-sound the gifts and graces which He has procured by

His death and bestowed on those who believe. He does this by the power of His resurrection through which He has conquered all our spiritual enemies. He continues to conquer them by His power, such that no one will be able to "snatch" His sheep from His hand (John 10:28).

Eighth, by His resurrection Christ raises our bodies from the grave on the day of judgment to eternal glory. But are not the wicked also raised by the power of Christ (Rom. 8:11)? Yes, but we must keep in mind that the power of Christ is twofold: the power of a Judge and the power of a Savior. By the first, Christ raises the ungodly from the dead. He executes on them the curse that was announced at the beginning of the world: "in the day that you eat of it you shall surely die" (Gen. 2:17). The second is the power of Christ's resurrection, and it belongs to Him as He is our Savior. By it He will raise to eternal life all those who by the bond of the Holy Spirit are mystically united to Him. By means of this union, this power will flow from the Head to the dead bodies of those who are in Christ.

Thus, we see what the power of Christ's resurrection is, and we see what Paul desires—namely, that he may experience these eight effects. Several important lessons arise from this point.

First, we learn that Christ's resurrection is the foundation of all comfort. By the power of His resurrection from death to life, all our spiritual enemies are conquered and subdued. Christ daily subdues them more and more in us. For this reason, He says, "These things I have spoken to you, that in Me you may have peace. In the world you will have tribulation; but be of good cheer, I have overcome the world" (John 16:33). This victory is for us, and it is made ours by faith. John says, "This is the victory that has overcome the world—our faith" (1 John 5:4).

Are you afraid on account of the prevalence of your sins, the cruelty of tyrants, the hatred of the world, the pain of hell, the suffering of death, or the temptation of the devil? Do not be dismayed, but rest in Christ by faith. He arose from death to life for you, and thereby shows Himself to be a Rock for you. In Him you will find sure remedies against all the troubles and miseries of life and death.

Second, we learn that we must rise with Christ from our sins and live to God in newness of life. Thus, we pray that we may feel the power of Christ's resurrection to change and renew us. We reap great benefits by this power, and we are to give thanks to God for them. We can only do this by newness of life. Christ arose for us, that we might rise to a new spiritual life from our sins and corruptions in which we are buried as in a grave (Rom. 6:4). The reward is great for those who make this change. "Blessed and holy is he who has part in the first resurrection. Over such the second death has no power" (Rev. 20:6). On the contrary, those who never rise from their sins and evil ways will certainly suffer the second death.

Third, we learn that the power of Christ's resurrection and the merit of His death are joined inseparably. This implies that those who do not find the power of Christ's resurrection to raise them to a holy and spiritual life that is acceptable to God, deceive themselves if they claim the merit of Christ's death in the remission of their sins. By rising, Christ put all our enemies under His feet, and "led captivity captive" (Eph. 4:8), even sin itself. It is, therefore, a shame for us to walk in the ways of sin and to make ourselves slaves and captives to it.

By arising from death, Christ made Himself a principal leader and guide to eternal life (Acts 3:15). It is wickedness to walk in the ways of our own heart, and not follow this heavenly guide. The care to keep a good conscience is a certain fruit and effect of Christ's resurrection. Thus, Peter says, "There is also an antitype which now saves us—baptism (not the removal of the filth of the flesh, but the answer of a good conscience toward God), through the resurrection of Jesus Christ" (1 Peter 3:21). The word "answer" implies an interrogation. The minister in the name of God demands whether we renounce the world, the flesh, and the devil, and take the true God for our God. In response, we demand of God whether He will promise to accept us, being wretched sinners, for His servants. And this is how we make profession of our thoughts and desires.

Fourth, we learn that we should submit ourselves to Christ. By the power of His resurrection, the earth trembled (Matt. 27:51), and thereby every creature professed its subjection and homage to Him. If we believe that Christ arose from the dead for us, then our hearts should tremble, and we should yield ourselves in subjection to Him in all obedience. Someone might say, "You bid us to rise from our sins as Christ rose to the glory of His Father. But this is wholly God's work in us, and not our work." That is true. Yet we can use the outward means of hearing and reading, and if we have any spark of grace, we can ask the Spirit of God to work this desire in us. God appoints exhortations and admonitions as means whereby He works in us that which He requires and commands. Therefore, let us listen to the voice of Christ. "Awake, you who sleep, arise from the dead, and Christ will give you light" (Eph. 5:14). Worldly cares must not hinder us in this work. Paul says, "If then you were raised with Christ, seek those things which are above, where Christ is, sitting at the right hand of God" (Col. 3:1).

Fifth, we learn that we should not be content with knowing Christ in the brain and speaking well of Him. We must go further, and labor to taste and feel by experience how good and sweet a Savior He is unto us, so that our hearts may be rooted and grounded in His love (Eph. 3:17–19). This was Paul's aim. We, too, must seek it through all possible means.

CHAPTER 17

The Fellowship of
Christ's Suffering

*That I may know Him and the power of His res-
urrection, and the fellowship of His sufferings, being
conformed to His death.*
                                    —Philippians 3:10

Paul desires not only to know "the power" of Christ's "resurrection," but "the fellowship of His sufferings." What
are the sufferings of Christ? They include not only the
sufferings which He endured in His person, but those
which are endured by His members. When Saul persecuted the church, it is said that he persecuted Christ
(Acts 9:4). This is why Paul writes, "I now rejoice in my
sufferings for you, and fill up in my flesh what is lack-
ing in the afflictions of Christ, for the sake of His body,
which is the church" (Col. 1:24).

If the members of the body of Christ suffer civil
or ecclesiastical punishments for doing evil, these are
not Christ's sufferings. Peter tells us, "But rejoice to the
extent that you partake of Christ's sufferings, that when

His glory is revealed, you may also be glad with exceeding joy. If you are reproached for the name of Christ, blessed are you, for the Spirit of glory and of God rests upon you. On their part He is blasphemed, but on your part He is glorified. But let none of you suffer as a murderer, a thief, an evildoer, or as a busybody in other people's matters" (1 Peter 4:13–15). Our sufferings are accounted to be the sufferings of Christ when they are experienced for a good cause and for the name of Christ.

What does it mean to have fellowship with Christ in His suffering? It is twofold. First, it is internal. It is the mortification of the flesh or the crucifying of the affections and their lusts. Second, it is external. It is the mortification of the outward man by various afflictions. Paul speaks of this in our text. Fellowship with Christ in His death is our conformity to His suffering and death.

It is worth recognizing what this conformity is not. God poured out the whole curse of the law, due to our sins, upon Christ. By this means He showed Christ justice without mercy. But in our afflictions God moderates His anger, and in justice He remembers mercy (Hab. 3:2). He lays no more on us than we can bear (1 Cor. 10:13). Furthermore, Christ's sufferings are a satisfaction to God's justice for our sins. Our sufferings are not so. We stand before God as private persons, and for this cause the sufferings of one man cannot satisfy for another, and there is no proportion between our sufferings and the glory which will be revealed (Rom. 8:17). As Christ says, "I have trodden the winepress alone" (Isa. 63:3).

And so, how are we conformed to Christ's suffering? It stands in four things. First, Christ suffered for a just cause, for He suffered as our Redeemer, the righteous for the unrighteous (1 Peter 3:18). We must likewise suffer for the sake of righteousness (Matt. 5:10).

Second, in His sufferings Christ was a mirror of all patience and meekness. "For to this you were called, because Christ also suffered for us, leaving us an example, that you should follow His steps: 'Who committed no sin, nor was deceit found in His mouth'" (1 Peter 2:21–22). We must show the same patience in our sufferings. For this to happen, our patience must possess three properties. (1) It must be voluntary. We must willingly and quietly renounce our own wills, and subject ourselves in our sufferings to God's will. Forced patience is not patience. (2) It must be singular. We must suffer not for praise or profit, but for the glory of God. We suffer to show our obedience to Him. (3) It must be constant. If we endure afflictions for a season, but later begin to complain and cast away Christ's yoke, we fail in our patience. The affections of grief and sorrow are compatible with patience, for Christian religion does not abolish these affections, but moderates them by bringing them into subjection to God's will when we lie under the cross.

Third, we are conformed to Christ's suffering when we learn obedience. "Though He was a Son, yet He learned obedience by the things which He suffered. And having been perfected, He became the author of eternal salvation to all who obey Him" (Heb. 5:8–9). Christ was not a sinner who had to learn to obey. Rather, He experienced obedience as a righteous man. Likewise, we must be careful to seek the fruit of our sufferings rather than their removal. This fruit is to learn obedience, especially to obey God's commands to believe and repent. God afflicted Job, not on account of his sins, but to test his faith and patience. In the end Job renewed his repentance: "Therefore I abhor myself, and repent in dust and ashes" (Job 42:6). Paul says that he received in his own flesh "the sentence of death" that he might learn to trust in God alone (2 Cor. 1:9).

Fourth, we are conformed to Christ in His suffering when it is even to death itself. We must resist sin, fighting against it to the shedding of our blood (Heb. 12:4). Faith and a good conscience are more precious than the blood of our hearts. Therefore, if necessary, we must conform ourselves to Christ, even in the pains of death.

This is the conformity of which Paul speaks. He magnifies it as a special gain. Why? First, it is a mark of God's children. "If you endure chastening, God deals with you as with sons; for what son is there whom a father does not chasten?" (Heb. 12:7). Second, it is a sign that the Holy Spirit dwells in us. "If you are reproached for the name of Christ, blessed are you, for the Spirit of glory and of God rests upon you" (1 Peter 4:14). Third, the grace of God is manifested most in afflictions: "My strength is made perfect in weakness" (2 Cor. 12:9). "Tribulation produces perseverance" (Rom. 5:3), because then "the love of God has been poured out in our hearts by the Holy Spirit who was given to us" (v. 5). Hope of eternal life shows itself most in the patient bearing of afflictions (Rom. 15:4–5). In times of ease and peace, natural life reigns. But in seasons of suffering natural life quickly decays, and the spiritual life of Christ shows itself. Fourth, conformity to Christ in His death is the right and certain way to eternal life. "We must through many tribulations enter the kingdom of God" (Acts 14:22). "This is a faithful saying: For if we died with Him, we shall also live with Him. If we endure, we shall also reign with Him" (2 Tim. 2:11–12). The estate of humiliation is the way to the estate of exaltation, first in Christ and then in us.

What do we learn from this?

First, we learn that after believers are made partakers of Christ and His benefits by the power of His resurrection, they must be made conformable to His death. Christ's commandment to those who would be His disciples is this: "If anyone desires to come after Me, let him deny himself, and take up his cross daily, and follow Me. For whoever desires to save his life will lose it, but whoever loses his life for My sake will save it" (Luke 9:23–24). There are three weighty reasons why God will have it so: (1) that He may correct past sins; (2) that He may prevent future sins; (3) that He may test what is in our hearts.

Second, we learn that there is comfort in our sufferings. We are partners with Christ in our sufferings, and He promises to make us His fellows. It follows that all our afflictions are well-known to Christ, and that they are laid on us with His consent. For this cause, we should frame ourselves to bear them with all meekness. As our partner, Christ will help us to bear them by moderating their weight or by governing them for our good (Rom. 8:28).

Third, we learn that our afflictions are blessings and benefits. We can discern them to be such, not by the light of reason, but by the eye of faith, because they are means to make us conformable to our Head, Christ Jesus. God's benefits are positive and privative. Positive benefits are those which God bestows on us. Privative benefits occur when God takes away a blessing and gives another. This kind of benefit is an affliction. The first is more prevalent in the life to come, while the second is more prevalent in this life. Therefore, while we live in this world, our duty is to labor to attain this conformity to the sufferings of Christ.

CHAPTER 18
Eternal Glory

If, by any means, I may attain to the resurrection from the dead.
—Philippians 3:11

Here is the third degree in Paul's gain. By "resurrection," he has in view the reward of eternal life. The act itself of rising from the dead is not gain, for the resurrection is common to all, the just and the unjust (Acts 24:15). It is eternal life, following the resurrection, that is the reward.

The expression, "if, by any means," is a figure of speech. Paul is not suggesting that he has any doubt regarding the certainty of his resurrection, for he was persuaded that nothing could separate him from Christ (Rom. 8:38–39). Elsewhere, he declares that the resurrection of the body to eternal life is an essential article of the faith (2 Tim. 1:12; 2:18). In using this expression, Paul is simply acknowledging the difficulty in obtaining his desired gain. There are three "means" to come to eternal life. The first is by a peaceful life and death. The second is by a life filled with afflictions. The third is by a cruel and violent death. Paul's desire is to obtain the crown of eternal glory by any of these means. If not by the first or second, then by the third.

The Christian's gain is eternal glory. It is a certain state of life in which all the promises of God in Christ are applied to us in heaven. It will be better understood by answering two questions.

First, what will cease in eternal glory? Seven things. (1) The execution of Christ's mediatorship (or His offices of prophet, priest, and king) will cease. Paul teaches this when he says that, when the end comes, Christ "delivers the kingdom to God the Father" (1 Cor. 15:24). Though the execution of His mediatorship will then cease, believers will lack nothing because they will know the full and eternal fruition of all the benefits of redemption. (2) All callings in family, church, and country will cease. Christ then "puts an end to all rule and all authority and power" (1 Cor. 15:24). In this blessed estate, there will be no magistrate and people, master and servant, husband and wife, parents and children, pastor and people, but all outward distinctions will cease. We will be as the angels of God. (3) All virtues that pertain to us, as we are pilgrims here on earth, will cease. Faith, hope, and patience will end because we will obtain all the things for which we believe and hope. The part of prayer called petition will cease. So, too, will preaching and hearing the Word and using the sacraments (1 Cor. 13:8). (4) Original sin and its fruits will cease. No unclean thing will enter the heavenly Jerusalem. (5) All miseries and sorrows, and all infirmities of body and mind, will cease (Rev. 21:4). All defects in eyes, arms, and legs will be restored. (6) The natural life and its means (such as food, drink, clothing, medicine, and recreation) will cease. Our bodies will be spiritual—that is, immediately and eternally preserved by the operation of the Holy Spirit, as now the body of Christ is in heaven. (7) The vanity of the creatures will cease. At the last judgment, the heavens and earth will be restored to their former excellence (Acts 3:21).

Second, what will we enjoy in eternal glory? Three things. The first is immediate and eternal fellowship with God the Father, the Son, and the Holy Spirit (1 Cor. 15:28). In this happy estate the tabernacle of God will be with us. "And I heard a loud voice from heaven saying, 'Behold, the tabernacle of God is with men, and He will dwell with them, and they shall be His people. God Himself will be with them and be their God'" (Rev. 21:3). God will be all things that the heart can desire. Augustine says, "There will be exceeding peace in us and among us and with God Himself, because we will see Him and enjoy Him always in all places." Therefore, that life will be blessed, for we will enjoy God Himself. For the manner of our enjoying Him, we will enjoy Him by Himself without any other means. For the measure, we will enjoy Him fully. For the time, we will enjoy Him eternally. For the place, we will enjoy Him in heaven.

Lastly, for the companions in our enjoyment of God, they will be God's people. From this fruition of God will arise eternal and unspeakable joy. "In Your presence is fullness of joy; at Your right hand are pleasures forevermore" (Ps. 16:11). In the transfiguration of Christ, which was but a shadow of the eternal glory, Peter was ravished with joy and delight (Matt. 17:5–6). The joy of heaven, therefore, will be unspeakable.

The second thing that we will enjoy is glorification in mind and body. We will be glorified in mind because we will then be partakers of the divine nature—that is, divine virtues and qualities (2 Peter 1:4). Our thoughts will be more excellent than those which God bestowed on Adam. We will be glorified in body because it will be made like the glorious body of Christ. He "will transform our lowly body that it may be conformed to His glorious body, according to the working by which He is able even to subdue all things to Himself" (Phil. 3:21).

The third thing that we will enjoy is dominion over heaven and earth. Adam lost this lordship at the fall, but it will be restored in glory. "He who overcomes shall inherit all things, and I will be his God and he shall be My son" (Rev. 21:7).

By considering these things, we have a taste of the excellence of this third gain: eternal glory.

CHAPTER 19

The Way to Eternal Life

*If, by any means, I may attain to the resurrection
from the dead.*

—Philippians 3:11

Here we see the third degree in Paul's gain: eternal glory,
which is a state of life in which all the promises of God
in Christ are applied to us in heaven. It is important to
note three details concerning this reward.

First, it is not easy to obtain the desired gain of eternal life. The reason is obvious: the way there is full of
impediments. First, "we do not wrestle against flesh and
blood, but against principalities, against powers, against
the rulers of the darkness of this age, against spiritual
hosts of wickedness in the heavenly places" (Eph. 6:12).
These seek the destruction of our souls. Second, innu-
merable lusts surround us, press us down, and draw us
away to the broad way of destruction (Heb. 12:1; James
1:14). Third, false doctrines and evil examples tempt us to

fall away from the faith. Fourth, we encounter manifold tribulations from beginning to end (Rom. 8:35).

Hence, we learn that we must give all diligence that we may attain to the reward of glory. We must struggle, strive, and wrestle to enter at the straight gate (Matt. 7:13). The principal gain, and the difficulty in obtaining it, requires our principal study and labor. Therefore, those who use no means, but leave all to God, thinking it the easiest matter in the world to win the kingdom of heaven, act wickedly. Those who profess religion in a slack and negligent manner, being neither hot nor cold, also act wickedly.

Second, Paul's desire for eternal glory shaped his present life. Some people might think that wicked people have the same desire for glory. But the difference is that in Paul there was an endeavor answerable to his desire. He says that he has "hope in God…that there will be a resurrection of the dead, both of the just and the unjust. This being so, I myself always strive to have a conscience without offense toward God and men" (Acts 24:15–16). The ungodly have no such desire, and therefore their lives yield no fruit. Being justified by faith, Paul desires to attain to full fellowship with Christ and to conformity with Him in glory. The same desire and endeavor should be in us.

Third, Paul is content to endure any kind of death, even a cruel death, to obtain the reward of eternal life. He is an example of courage. "For God has not given us a spirit of fear, but of power and of love and of a sound mind" (2 Tim. 1:7). The courage of Moses was the same. He was content to endure affliction with God's people, "for he looked to the reward" (Heb. 11:25–26). The courage of the martyrs was the same. They "were tortured, not accepting deliverance, that they might obtain a better resurrection" (v. 35). Walking in the way to eternal life, we must show the same courage in all dangers. For this reason, we must pray to God to give us the Spirit of courage, and we must always attend upon the commandments of God, making them the foundation of our courage. We must also rest upon the promise of God's presence and protection.

If it is said that we are by nature fearful in dangers, and therefore incapable of courage, we must be careful to acknowledge that there is a threefold fear. The first is the fear of human nature. We eschew that which is hurtful to us. This fear was in Christ, whose soul was heavy unto death (Heb. 5:7). He feared the curse of death which He endured. Such fear is not a sin, and it may stand with courage. The second is the fear of corrupt human nature. It occurs when a person fears without cause or measure. The disciples feared without cause when they saw Christ walking upon the sea (Matt. 14:26). Some people fear without measure when, distrusting God, they neglect their calling or their duty to pray in time of danger. This kind of fear is an enemy to all true courage. The third is when danger and death are indeed feared, but it is ordered by faith and hope in the mercy and providence of God, and it is joined with obedience to God. This proceeds from grace, and it may stand with courage, and it serves to order the two former fears.

CHAPTER 20

Knowing Christ Crucified

Yet indeed I also count all things loss for the excellence of the knowledge of Christ Jesus my Lord, for whom I have suffered the loss of all things, and count them as rubbish, that I may gain Christ.
—Philippians 3:8

It is a common sin in our day that people do not know Christ as they should. The right knowledge of Christ is not speaking frequently of His death and resurrection, or calling Him "Savior," or handling the mystery of the incarnation biblically and faithfully (though that is a worthy gift of God). So, what is it?

First, it is to be touched with a lively feeling of our sins, for which our Redeemer suffered the pain of hell. It is to dislike ourselves and our past lives on account of our sins, and to purpose to reform ourselves and seek greater conformity to Christ in all good duties. Second, it is to behold His passion, to comprehend the length, breadth, height, and depth of the love of God (Eph. 3:18–19), who gave His Son for us upon the cross. Third, it is to marvel at the goodness of the Son of God who loved His enemies more than Himself, whereby our hearts are rooted and grounded in His love and inflamed in love to God (Eph. 3:17).

Paul declares, "I determined not to know anything among you except Jesus Christ and Him crucified" (1 Cor. 2:2). It is the most excellent and worthy part of divine wisdom to know Christ crucified. The prophet Isaiah says, "By His knowledge [that is, Christ crucified] My righteous Servant shall justify many" (Isa. 53:11). Christ says, "And this is eternal life, that they may know You, the only true God, and Jesus Christ whom You have sent" (John 17:3). Paul proclaims, "But God forbid that I should boast except in the cross of our Lord Jesus Christ, by whom the world has been crucified to me, and I to the world" (Gal. 6:14).

We must know Christ, not generally and confusedly, for even the demons know Him like that (James 2:19), but we must know Him by a lively, powerful, and operative knowledge. Such knowledge requires three things.

The first is consideration, whereby we seriously conceive Christ as He is revealed in the gospel and as He is offered to us in the ministry of the Word and sacraments. Consideration includes two things. When we consider, we labor to feel our need of Christ crucified. We stand in desperate need of the least drop of His blood for the washing away of our sins. Unless we feel our need for all the grace and goodness that are in Christ, and feel our extreme need of His suffering, we will never learn Christ in truth. When we consider, we also long for participation in Christ. We cry out, "Shall I die of thirst?" (Judges 15:18). We long for our thirst to be satisfied in Christ.

The second requirement is application. We believe that Christ was crucified, and we believe that He was crucified for us personally. Here we must remember two truths.

First, Christ was our pledge and surety on the cross. He stood in the place in which we should have stood in our own persons. Our sins were imputed and applied to Him, and He stood guilty as a criminal for them, and suffered the very pains of hell. God accepts His sufferings as if we had borne the curse of the law in our own person eternally.

Believing this truth is the very foundation of religion. For this reason, we must be careful to apply Christ crucified to ourselves. When Elisha would revive the child of the Shunamite woman, he went up and lay upon him, and put his mouth upon his mouth, and his hands upon his hands, and his eyes upon his eyes, and stretched himself upon him (2 Kings 4:34). Even so, if we would be revived to eternal life, we must by faith (as it were) set ourselves upon the cross of Christ, and apply our hands to His hands, our feet to His feet, and our sinful heart to His bleeding heart. We must not be content, like

Thomas, to put our finger into Christ's side. Rather, we must plunge ourselves (body and soul) into His wounds and blood. This will make us cry with Thomas: "My Lord and my God!" (John 20:28).

This is what it means to be crucified with Christ. And yet, we do not stay here, but by faith we descend with Christ from the cross to the grave, and we bury ourselves in His burial. As the dead soldier tumbled into the grave of Elisha and was made alive upon touching his body (2 Kings 13:21), so by spiritually touching Christ we are quickened to eternal life.

The second truth to remember is that Christ crucified is ours. God the Father really gives Him to us, even as gifts are bestowed by earthly fathers upon their children. We must firmly believe this. It is in this way that Christ's benefits are indeed ours for our justification and salvation.

The third requirement to lively knowledge is affection. All the affections of our hearts must be carried to Christ, and thereby transformed into Him. He gave Himself for us, and we can do no less than set our hearts upon Him. We must love Him above all. We must value Him at so high a price that He must be to us better than ten thousand worlds. All those things which we enjoy must be as loss and rubbish to us in respect of Him. All our joy, comfort, and confidence must be placed in Him. It is merely a knowledge swimming in the brain that does not alter and dispose the affections toward Christ.

CHAPTER 21

Christ's Merit

And of His fullness we have all received, and grace
for grace.
— John 1:16

We have seen that we must know Christ with a lively, powerful, and operative knowledge. But what exactly must we know? In sum, Christ must be known as He is our Redeemer and the price of our redemption. In this respect, He must be considered as the treasury of God's church, as Paul testifies when he says, "In [Him] are hidden all the treasures of wisdom and knowledge" (Col. 2:3). Again, "Blessed be the God and Father of our Lord Jesus Christ, who has blessed us with every spiritual blessing in heavenly places in Christ" (Eph. 1:3). Similarly, John says, "Of His fullness we have all received, and grace for grace" (John 1:16). Let us note that all God's blessings, whether spiritual or material, all without exception, are conveyed to us from the Father through Christ. And we must receive them from Christ.

We receive three main blessings from Christ: His merit, His virtue, and His example. The first is the subject of this chapter.

What is the merit of Christ? It is the value of His death and obedience whereby we are perfectly reconciled to God. This reconciliation has two parts. The first is remission of sins. This is the removal of the guilt and punishment due our sin. Guilt is an obligation to punishment, according to the order of divine justice. Punishment is the curse of the whole law, which is the suffering of the first and second death. The second part of reconciliation is acceptance to eternal life. God gives us a right and title to the kingdom of heaven because of the merit of Christ's imputed obedience.

We must know this blessing of reconciliation, not by imagination or presumption, but by the inward testimony of the Holy Spirit who certifies it to our consciences (Rom. 8:15). For this reason, He is called "the Spirit of wisdom and revelation" (Eph. 1:17). To attain to an infallible assurance of this blessing, we must call to mind the promises of the gospel touching the remission of sins and the gift of eternal life. Then, we must endeavor by the assurance of the Holy Spirit to apply these promises to ourselves, and to believe that they belong to us. We must also pursue all the exercises of prayer and repentance. It is by crying to God for reconciliation that assurance comes, as Scripture makes manifest. If a person in temptation feels nothing but the indignation of God, against all reason and feeling, he must hold to the merit of Christ. He must learn a very hard point of religion—namely, God is a most loving Father to those who desire to serve Him, even when He shows Himself to be a most fierce enemy.

Four benefits proceed from the blessing of reconciliation. First, we receive the excellent "peace of God, which surpasses all understanding" (Phil. 4:7). It has six components. The first is peace with the blessed Trinity. "Therefore, having been justified by faith, we have peace with God through our Lord Jesus Christ" (Rom. 5:1).

The second is peace with the angels. "Most assuredly, I say to you, hereafter you shall see heaven open, and the angels of God ascending and descending upon the Son of Man" (John 1:51). As armies of soldiers, angels encamp about the servants of God and, as nurses, they bear them in their arms, so that they are not hurt by the devil or his instruments. Their ministry for us proceeds from the fact that, being in Christ, we are partakers of His merits.

The third component is peace with all those who fear God and believe in Christ. Isaiah foretold this when he said that "the wolf also shall dwell with the lamb, the leopard shall lie down with the young goat, the calf and the young lion and the fatling together; and a little child shall lead them" (Isa. 11:6).

The fourth component is peace with a person's own self, when the conscience is washed in the blood of

Christ, and it ceases to accuse and terrify. The affections and inclinations of the whole person are obedient to the mind enlightened by the Holy Spirit. "Let the peace of God rule in your hearts" (Col. 3:15).

The fifth component is peace with enemies. Those who believe in Christ seek to live at peace with all men, hurting none, but doing good to all. Moreover, God restrains the malice of enemies and inclines their hearts to be peaceable. Thus, God brought Daniel "into the favor and goodwill of the chief of the eunuchs" (Dan. 1:9).

The sixth and final component is peace with all creatures in heaven and earth, in that they serve for our salvation. "You shall tread upon the lion and the cobra, the young lion and the serpent you shall trample underfoot" (Ps. 91:13). "In that day I will make a covenant for them with the beasts of the field, with the birds of the air, and with the creeping things of the ground" (Hosea 2:18).

This benefit of peace is known partly by the testimony of the Holy Spirit and partly by our daily experience of it.

CHAPTER 22

An Interest in Christ's Merit

Whether...the world or life or death, or things present or things to come—all are yours.
—1 Corinthians 3:22

Four benefits proceed from the blessing of reconciliation. The first was handled in the last chapter: we receive "the peace of God" (Phil. 4:7). The remaining three are the focus of this chapter.

The first benefit is the recovery of a right and title to all creatures in heaven and earth and all temporal blessings. Adam lost this right for himself and all his posterity when he sinned in the garden. But now, it is restored to us in Christ. Hence, Paul can say, "Whether...the world or life or death, or things present or things to come—all are yours" (1 Cor. 3:22). The right way to appreciate this benefit is as follows. When God promises food, drink, clothing, houses, lands, and so forth, we must not merely consider them as His blessings, for even unbelievers can do that. We must esteem them as blessings which proceed from His special love, whereby He loves us in Christ. He procured these blessings for us by the merit of Christ crucified. We must labor to be persuaded of this. As often as we use the creatures of God for our own benefit, this point should come to our minds. Blessings conceived apart from Christ are misconceived. Whatever they are in themselves, they are only blessings to us in and by Christ's merit.

Therefore, we must observe the following order touching earthly blessings. First, we must have an interest in Christ's merit. Second, by means of His merit, we have a right before God to use the things we enjoy. All those who use the creatures of God as His gifts, but do not use them by Christ's merit, do so as usurpers and thieves. For this reason, it is not sufficient for us to know (generally and confusedly) Christ to be our Redeemer, but we must learn to see, know, and acknowledge Him in every specific gift and blessing of God. When eating and drinking, we should behold these gifts by the eye of faith and see in them the merit of Christ's passion. If we were able to do this, there would not be so much greed, excess, or drunkenness. If people would consider their houses, lands, possessions, etc., as blessings that come to them by the fountain of blessing, the merit of Christ, there would not be so much fraud and deceit, so much injustice and oppression.

That which I have just said of food, drink, clothing,

and belongings, must also be understood of status and position. A noble birth and upbringing, without a new birth in Christ, is an earthly vanity (Col. 2:10; 3:11). The same may be said of medicine, sleep, health, liberty, and even our breathing the air. Likewise, Christ must be known in our recreation. All recreation involves the use of indifferent things, and the holy use of all indifferent things is purchased to us by the blood of Christ. For this reason, it is very suitable that Christian men and women should join meditation on the death of Christ with their recreation. If this were practiced, there would not be so many unlawful sports, delights, and frivolities, nor so much abuse of lawful recreation.

The second benefit is that crosses, afflictions, and judgments are no longer curses and punishments for those who are in Christ. They are only means of trial and correction. Christ's death has taken away the curse of the law. For this reason, we must see our afflictions as trials or chastisements, proceeding from the hand of a bountiful and loving Father. We must view them in and through the merit of Christ. If we regard them in any other way, as proceeding from a vengeful Judge, then we will see them as curses and punishments for sin. All of this means that subjection to God's hand in all crosses is a mark and badge of the true church.

The last benefit is that death is now a rest or sleep (1 Thess. 4:13). We must consider death, not as it is set forth in the law, but as it is altered by Christ's death

(1 Cor. 15:55). When death comes, we must look at it through Christ's death, as through a glass. When we do, it will appear as nothing more than a passage from this life to eternal life.

CHAPTER 23

Christ's Virtue

For to me, to live is Christ, and to die is gain.
—Philippians 1:21

Because Christ is our Redeemer and the price of our redemption, all blessings, without exception, are communicated from the Father through Christ to us. These include His merit, His virtue, and His example. Having expounded the first, we turn our attention to the second. Christ's virtue is the power of His Godhead whereby He creates new hearts in all those who believe in Him, and He makes them new creatures. This virtue is twofold.

First, it is the virtue of Christ's death whereby He freed Himself from the punishment and imputation of our sins. The same virtue serves to mortify the corruptions of our minds, wills, and affections, even as a corrosive consumes the rotten flesh in any part of the body.

Second, it is the virtue of Christ's resurrection. This is the power of His Godhead whereby He raised

Himself from death to life. The same power serves to raise those who belong to Christ from their sins in this life and from the grave on the day of the last judgment.

The knowledge of this double virtue must not be speculative (that is, merely conceived in the brain), but experimental. We ought to have experience of it in our hearts and lives. We should labor by all possible means to feel the power of Christ's death in killing our sins, and the virtue of His resurrection in putting spiritual life into us, that we might be able to say that we no longer live but Christ lives in us (Gal. 2:20). This was one of the most excellent and principal things for which Paul sought. He desired to "know Him and the power of His resurrection" (Phil. 3:10).

Conformity to Christ in His spiritual life consists of four parts. The first is conformity to His offering. In the garden and on the cross, Christ prayed with strong cries and tears (Heb. 5:7). He presented Himself as a sacrifice of propitiation to God's offended justice (Rom. 3:25). Similarly, we must present and offer ourselves (body and soul), and all we have, to God's service in our calling as a Christian and in our specific vocation in which He has placed us (Rom. 12:1; 1 Cor. 7:20–24). David says, "Sacrifice and offering You did not desire; my ears You have opened. Burnt offering and sin offering You did not require. Then I said, 'Behold, I come; in the scroll of the book it is written of me. I delight to do Your will, O my God, and Your law is within my heart'" (Ps. 40:6–8).

The second part is conformity to Christ's crucifixion. First, as He bore His cross to the place of execution, so we must (as good disciples of Christ) deny ourselves, take up all the crosses and afflictions that God lays upon us, and follow Him (Matt. 16:24). Second, we must become like Him in crucifying the body of sin. "And those who are Christ's have crucified the flesh with its passions and desires" (Gal. 5:24). By the sword of the Spirit, we must wound sin to death (Eph. 6:17). This being done, we must labor to see and feel its death, and to lay it (so to speak) in a grave, so that it never rises again. Then, we should daily cast new dirt over it.

The third part of conformity to Christ's spiritual life is conformity to His resurrection. As Christ arose from death, we should by God's grace use means so that we may increasingly come out of our sins, as out of a repugnant grave, to live to God in newness of life. It is difficult for us to come out of the grave of our sins, and it can only be done by degrees as God gives grace. We must begin by stirring ourselves, as a person who comes out of unconsciousness, awakened by the voice of Christ sounding in his deaf ears. Next, we must raise up our minds to a better condition. After this, we must lift one hand out of the grave, followed by the other. Once done, we must put one foot out of the grave, followed by the other. Our hope is that on the day of judgment we will be wholly delivered from all bonds of corruption.

The fourth part of conformity to Christ's spiritual life is conformity to His ascension. As He ascended into heaven, we continually elevate our hearts and minds to Christ who sits at the right hand of the Father. As Paul says, "For our citizenship is in heaven, from which we also eagerly wait for the Savior, the Lord Jesus Christ" (Phil. 3:20). Again, "If then you were raised with Christ, seek those things which are above, where Christ is, sitting at the right hand of God" (Col. 3:1).

CHAPTER 24

Christ's Example

Take My yoke upon you and learn from Me, for I am gentle and lowly in heart.

—Matthew 11:29

All God's blessings, whether spiritual or material, are conveyed to us from the Father by Christ. We have looked at His merit and virtue. The remaining blessing is His example. We deceive ourselves if we think that Christ is only to be known as a Redeemer and not as a pattern of all good duties, to which we ought to be conformed. Indeed, we must follow the example of the servants of God here on earth, but we do so only so far as they imitate Christ. We follow Him in the practice of every good duty, without exception (1 Cor. 11:1).

Conformity to Christ in moral duties is either general or special. General conformity to Him is to be holy as He is holy (1 Peter 1:16). "For whom He foreknew, He also predestined to be conformed to the image of His Son, that He might be the firstborn among many brethren" (Rom. 8:29). We are conformed to His image, not only in the cross, but also in holiness and glory. "And everyone who has this hope in Him purifies himself, just as He is pure" (1 John 3:3).

Special conformity to Christ is chiefly found in four virtues. The first is faith. When Christ bore the wrath of God, and the very pains of hell were upon Him, He depended upon the assistance, protection, and good pleasure of His Father (1 Peter 2:23). So, we must by a true and lively faith depend wholly upon God's mercy in Christ, in times of peace and trouble, in life and death. We must never let go, even if we should feel as though we descend to hell.

The second is meekness. "Take My yoke upon you and learn from Me, for I am gentle and lowly in heart" (Matt. 11:29). Christ showed His meekness in patiently bearing all injuries and abuses offered by the hands of wretched sinners, and in suffering the curse of the law, without complaining or grumbling, and with submission to His Father's will. The more we follow Him in this, the more we will be conformable to Him in His death and suffering (Phil. 3:10).

The third is love. "And walk in love, as Christ also has loved us and given Himself for us, an offering and a sacrifice to God for a sweet-smelling aroma" (Eph. 5:2). We ought to show the same love by serving all people within the scope of our callings and by being all things to all, so that we might do them all the good we can in body and soul. "For though I am free from all men, I have made myself a servant to all, that I might win the more" (1 Cor. 9:19).

The fourth is humility. Christ is a wonderful example of humility. Being God, He became man for us, and He became a worm, trodden under foot, that He might save us. "Let this mind be in you which was also in Christ Jesus, who, being in the form of God, did not consider it robbery to be equal with God, but made Himself of no reputation, taking the form of a bondservant, and coming in the likeness of men" (Phil. 2:5–7).

Here we must observe that there is something more in the example of Christ. He does not only show us what we ought to do, but His example serves as a remedy against vices and as a motive to pursue good duties.

First, the consideration that the Son of God suffered all the pains and torments of hell on the cross for our sins is the most effectual means to stir up our hearts to a godly sorrow for our sins. For this to happen, we must be convinced that we crucified Christ, that we are to blame (along with Judas, Herod, Pilate, and the Jews), and that our sins were the nails, spears, and thorns that pierced Him. When this realization begins to take root, we begin to experience poverty of spirit with mourning. "And I will pour on the house of David and on the inhabitants of Jerusalem the Spirit of grace and supplication; then they will look on Me whom they have pierced. Yes, they will mourn for Him as one mourns for his only son, and grieve for Him as one grieves for a firstborn" (Zech. 12:10).

In his first sermon, Peter struck the Jews with a thunderclap from heaven when he said to them: "Therefore let all the house of Israel know assuredly that God has made this Jesus, whom you crucified, both Lord and Christ" (Acts 2:36). In response, three thousand men "were cut to the heart, and said…'What shall we do?'" (v. 37). If Christ shed His blood for our sins, and if our sins made Him sweat water and blood, then surely, we should shed bitter tears for them. He who is so hardened that the passion of Christ does not humble him is in a lamentable condition.

Second, meditation on the suffering of Christ is a notable means to stir repentance and reformation of life. When we appreciate that Christ, by suffering the first and second death, has procured remission of all our sins, and freed us from hell, death, and damnation, then (if there is but a spark of grace in us) we begin to esteem His goodness. Has the Lord been so merciful to me (a firebrand of hell) as to free me from destruction and receive me in Christ? Blessed be His name! I will not, therefore, sin as I have done, but I will endeavor to keep myself from every evil way. Thus, faith purifies both heart and life.

Third, when you are in any pain or sickness, think of how light these are compared to the agony and bloody sweat, to the thorns and nails, of Christ. When you are wronged in word or deed, turn your eyes to the cross, consider how meekly He suffered all abuses in silence, and prayed for those who crucified Him. When you are tempted with pride, consider how Christ was despised, mocked, and condemned. When anger and malice inflame your heart, think how Christ gave Himself to save His enemies, even then when they did most cruelly mistreat Him. By these meditations, mingled with faith, your mind will be eased.

CHAPTER 25

A Threefold Knowledge

*That I may know Him and the power of His res-
urrection, and the fellowship of His sufferings, being
conformed to His death.*
                                                    —Philippians 3:10

We have seen that Christ is to be known as our
Redeemer and as the price of our redemption. All God's
blessings come to us through Him—His merit, His virtue, and His example. This knowledge of Christ crucified
is essential to knowing God, our neighbor, and ourselves.

First, the right knowledge of God arises from the
knowledge of Christ crucified. If we would know God
aright, and know Him to be our salvation, then we
must know Him only in Christ crucified. God in His
own majesty is invisible, not only to our eyes but to our
mind (1 Tim. 1:17). He is only revealed to us in Christ,
in whom He is to be seen as in a glass. In Christ He
sets forth His justice, goodness, wisdom, etc. For this
cause, Christ is called the "brightness of His glory and

the express image of His person" (Heb. 1:3). He is also called "the image of the invisible God" (Col. 1:15). Therefore, we must not seek to know God anywhere else but in Christ. Whatever is conceived of God apart from Christ is an idol of the brain.

Second, the right knowledge of neighbor arises from the knowledge of Christ crucified. When we do any duty for others, especially those who are part of God's church, we must not merely respect their persons, but Christ crucified in them and them in Christ. When Saul persecuted those who called on the name of Christ, Christ cried, "Saul, Saul, why are you persecuting Me?" (Acts 9:4). When a poor man comes to us for relief, it is Christ who comes to our door and says, "I am hungry. I am thirsty. I am naked." Let us be compassionate toward them as we would be toward Christ. If not, we will hear that fearful sentence on the day of judgment: "Depart from Me, you cursed, into the everlasting fire prepared for the devil and his angels: for I was hungry and you gave Me no food; I was thirsty and you gave Me no drink; I was a stranger and you did not take Me in, naked and you did not clothe Me, sick and in prison and you did not visit Me" (Matt. 25:41–43).

Third, the right knowledge of self arises from the knowledge of Christ crucified. First, we learn that our sins are grievous, and that our condition is therefore miserable. If we consider our offences in themselves, we may be deceived because the conscience is corrupt and often errs in giving testimony. It makes sin to appear less than it is. But if sin is considered in the death and suffering of Christ, of which it was the cause, then we see what it truly is. Its vileness is measured by the unspeakable torments endured by the Son of God. If the greatness of our sin is esteemed according to the endless satisfaction made to the justice of God, the least sin will appear to be most grievous. Therefore, we must see Christ crucified, so that we have a full view of what we are by nature.

What does this teach us?

First, we learn that we are not our own lords, but wholly (body and soul) belong to Christ. God the Father gives us to Christ, and He has purchased us with His own blood. "And you are Christ's, and Christ is God's" (1 Cor. 3:23). Hence, it comes to pass that Christ esteems all the crosses and afflictions of His people as His own. We must learn to give up ourselves (body and soul) to the honor and service of Christ.

Second, we learn that we (as new creatures in Christ) have our being and subsisting from Christ. "For we are members of His body, of His flesh and of His bones" (Eph. 5:30). In these words, Paul alludes to Adam's words concerning Eve: "This is now bone of my bones and flesh of my flesh" (Gen. 2:23). As Eve was made from a rib taken from Adam's side, so the whole church of God springs and arises out of the blood that streamed from the side of Christ crucified.

Third, we learn that all our good works proceed

from the merit of Christ crucified. He is the cause of them in us, and we are the causes of them in and by Him. Christ declares, "Without Me you can do nothing" (John 15:5).

Fourth, we learn that we owe an endless debt to Christ. He was crucified as our surety and pledge, and in the spectacle of His passion we must consider ourselves as the chief debtors. The very discharge of our debt (that is, the sins which are inherent in us) was the proper cause of all the endless pains and torments that Christ endured, that He might set us at liberty from hell, death, and damnation. When we think of His unspeakable goodness, we must confess that we owe ourselves (body and soul), and all that we have, as a debt to Him.

CHAPTER 26

Applying Christ and His Merits

Christ is all and in all.
—Colossians 3:11

We do not need to examine whether this manner of knowing Christ is found in the world. It is not. The Muslims acknowledge Him as nothing more than a prophet. The Jews scorn Him for His cross and suffering. Though the Roman Catholics confess Him in word, they do not know Him as they ought. They deface Christ crucified by insisting that the suffering of the martyrs is meritorious, and that the Virgin Mary is the queen of heaven and mother of mercy who may command Christ to forgive sins. They also give religious adoration to crucifixes made by human hands.

Common Protestants also fall short of the true manner of knowing Christ. How so? First, they acknowledge Him to be their Savior while insisting that He tolerates their sins. They walk in evil ways, yet persuade themselves that God is merciful, and that Christ has freed them from death and damnation. Second, they assume that a mere knowledge of Christ's suffering for the remission of sins is sufficient. But they have no regard for the virtue of Christ's death in the mortification of sin, or of the blessed example of His suffering. Third, they are content to know Christ to be their Redeemer, but never once seek to feel the benefit of His passion in every condition of life.

Why is it that most of the world lives in security, untouched by their horrible sins? Surely, it is because they never seriously consider that Christ in the garden lay groveling upon the earth, sweating water and blood, for their sins. Whatever they say in word, the tenor of their lives demonstrates that they are enemies of the cross of Christ, and that they tread His precious blood under their feet (Heb. 10:29).

Considering that this weighty point of religion is so neglected, we must seek to know Christ crucified. That we may attain to it, we must behold Him in the preaching of the Word and in the sacraments, in which we will see Him crucified before our eyes (Gal. 3:1). We do not seek to behold Him here with the eye of the body, but with the eye of true faith, applying Him and His merits to us, and we do so with a broken and bruised heart.

First, we behold Him as a glass, in which we see God's glory greater in our redemption than in our creation. In creation God's infinite wisdom, power, and goodness appeared, but in redemption His endless justice and mercy appeared. In creation we are members of the first Adam and bear his image, but in redemption we are members of the second Adam. In creation, we are endued with natural life, but in redemption with spiritual life. In creation, God gave life by commanding that to be which was not, but in redemption He gives not by life but by death, even the death of His Son. This is the mystery into which the angels desire to look (1 Peter 1:12).

Second, we behold Him as the full price of our redemption and perfect reconciliation with God and pray earnestly to God that He would seal it in our conscience by His Holy Spirit.

Third, we must behold Christ as an example, to whom we must conform ourselves. For this cause, we strive to say by experience that we are dead, crucified, and buried with Him, that we rise again with Him to newness of life, that He enlightens our minds and reforms our wills and affections, and that He gives us both the will and the deed in every good thing.

If we would behold God, we must look upon Him in Christ crucified. He is the express image of the Father's person. It is a terrible thing, when our conscience is troubled, to think of God without Christ. The glory of God in His endless mercy is seen in the face of Christ (2 Cor. 4:6). If we would come to God for grace, comfort, salvation, any blessing, we must first come to Christ hanging, bleeding, dying upon the cross, without whom there is no hearing God, no helping God, no saving God, no God to us at all. In a word, we must let Christ be all things unto us (Col. 3:11).

CHAPTER 27

Seeing Christ Crucified

*For I determined not to know anything among you
except Jesus Christ and Him crucified.*
—1 Corinthians 2:2

The knowledge of Christ crucified is our greatest need.
For this reason, we must read the gospel accounts of His
passion, and carefully observe all its parts and circum-
stances, and apply them to ourselves.

When we read that Christ went to the garden where
the Jews might arrest Him, we should consider that He
went willingly to the cross. He did so for our sins. Therefore, we should serve Him freely and willingly (Ps. 110:3).

When we read that Christ's soul was heavy unto
death, we should consider that it was for our sins. We
should be heavy in heart for sin. We should also see that
His sorrow is our joy if we believe in Him. "Rejoice in
the Lord always. Again I will say, rejoice!" (Phil. 4:4).

When we read that Christ prayed, groveling on the
ground, sweating water and blood, we should consider

the measure of God's wrath that was upon Him. It prostrated His body to the earth and caused His blood to flow. Our sins must be heinous if they brought such grievous pain to Christ. Is it not a shame for us to indulge in pride, wallow in pleasure, and neglect our poor brothers and sisters for whom Christ sweated water and blood? We should set aside the pride of our hearts, and be ashamed, and grieve in hearts, even bleed for our own offences, humbling ourselves with Ezra, saying, "O my God, I am too ashamed and humiliated to lift up my face to You, my God; for our iniquities have risen higher than our heads, and our guilt has grown up to the heavens" (Ezra 9:6).

When we read that Christ was taken and bound, we should consider that it was our sins that brought Him into the power of His enemies. We are bound with the chains of our own sins. By nature, our affections are chained to the will of the devil, so as we cannot do anything but what he wills. The bonds of Christ serve to purchase our liberty from hell, death, and damnation.

When we read that Christ was brought before Annas and Caiaphas, we should consider that the eternal Son of God, the sovereign Judge of the world, stood to be judged by wicked men. We should persuade ourselves that this great injustice is on account of our sins, humble ourselves in dust and ashes, and ask God to soften our stony hearts that we may turn to Him, and by true faith lay hold on Christ who has so abased Himself that His humiliation might be our glory and His prosecution our perfect absolution.

When we read that Barabbas, the murderer, was preferred before Christ who exceeds humans and angels in holiness, we should consider that it was our sins that placed this shameful reproach upon Him. We should remember that He was esteemed worse than Barabbas on our account, and therefore we see ourselves as most heinous and wretched sinners (1 Tim. 1:15).

When we read that Christ was condemned to the cursed death of the cross, we should consider God's wrath and fury against sin, and His great and infinite mercy to sinners. We should look at ourselves, and cry out, "I have sinned. I am guilty and worthy of damnation. But Your blessed Son stood in my room. Unspeakable mercy! I am a wretch. How long have I neglected You! O Son of God, how long have You abased Yourself for me? Therefore, give me grace, O God, that by beholding my estate in the person of Christ crucified, I might detest my sins that caused His suffering. Give me grace that by a lively faith I might embrace the forgiveness that You offer in Your Son. O Christ, Savior of the world, give me Your holy and blessed Spirit that I may judge myself, and be as vile and base in my eyes as You were vile before the Jews. Unite me to You by the same Spirit, that in You I may be as worthy to be accepted before God as I am worthy in myself to be detested for my sins."

When we read that Christ was clothed in purple and crowned with thorns, mocked and ridiculed, we should consider the everlasting shame that is due unto us. We should conform ourselves to Christ, and be content to be reproached, abused, and despised, so long as it is for a good cause.

When we read that Christ was stripped of all His clothes, we should consider that He was naked to bear our shame on the cross, and with His most precious and rich nakedness He covers our deformity.

When we read the complaint of Christ, that He was forsaken by His Father, we should consider how He suffered the pains and torments of hell as our pledge and surety. We learn by His unspeakable torments what a fearful thing it is to sin against God, and we begin to renounce ourselves and detest our sins, and walk as children of light, according to the measure of grace received. When we come to die, we set before our eyes Christ amid all His torments on the cross. In beholding this to our endless comfort, we see a paradise amid hell: God the Father reconciled to us, our Savior reaching out His hands to us to receive our souls unto Him, and His cross as a ladder to advance us to eternal glory. When He cried aloud with a strong voice at the point of death, it was to show that He died willingly without violence or constraint from any creature. If it had so pleased Him, He could have freed Himself from death, and have cast His enemies to the bottom of hell.

When we read that Christ commended His soul into the hands of His Father, we should consider that our souls are delivered up into the hands of God, and that we will be preserved against the rage and malice of all our enemies. Hence, we may be bold to commend our spirits into the hands of God the Father.

When we read of Christ's death, we should consider that our sins were its cause. We would have suffered death eternally if the Son of God had not come in our place. His death is a ransom to be apprehended by faith as the means of life. By death Christ has wounded both the first and second death, and He has made His cross to be a tribunal seat of judgment against all His enemies.

When we read of the trembling of the earth at Christ's death, we should consider that it groaned under the burden of sins in the world. By its motion it signified that even we deserved to be swallowed by the earth and to go down into the pit alive rather than to have any part in the merit of Christ crucified.

When we read of Christ's burial, we should consider that it was to ratify His death, and to vanquish death even in its own den. We apply this burial to ourselves and believe that it serves to make our graves a soft bed, and to free our bodies from corruption. We pray to God that we may feel the power of the Spirit of Christ, weakening and consuming the body of sin, even as a dead corpse rots in the grave, until it is dissolved to dust.

When we have thus applied Christ's death and suffering to ourselves, we labor by faith to see Him crucified in all the works of God either in us or upon us. We behold Him at our table in food and drink, which is a lively sermon and a daily pledge of God's mercy in Christ. We behold Him in all our afflictions as our partner who pities our case and has compassion on us. We behold Him in our most dangerous temptations in which the devil thunders damnation. We behold Him as a mighty Samson, bearing away the gates of His enemies upon His own shoulders, and killing more by death than by life, crucifying the devil even when He is crucified. We behold Him, by death killing death, by entrance into the grave opening the grave and giving life to the dead, and in the house of death spoiling the devil of all his strength and power. We behold Him in all the afflictions of our brothers and sisters, as though He were naked, hungry, sick, and we do all the good we can to them, as to Christ Himself.

Conclusion

Whoever comes to Me, and hears My sayings and does them, I will show you whom he is like: He is like a man building a house, who dug deep and laid the foundation on the rock. And when the flood arose, the stream beat vehemently against that house, and could not shake it, for it was founded on the rock.

—Luke 6:47–48

The foundation upon which we build is Christ alone (Eph. 2:20–21). "Nor is there salvation in any other, for there is no other name under heaven given among men by which we must be saved" (Acts 4:12). "For no other foundation can anyone lay than that which is laid, which is Jesus Christ" (1 Cor. 3:11). We build on Christ by believing in Him. As mutual love joins one man to another, so true faith makes us one with Christ (Eph. 3:17). "Those who trust in the LORD are like Mount Zion, which cannot be removed, but abides forever" (Ps. 125:1). As for our works, they are fruits, but they have no part in this foundation.

Christ is a Rock, but only as He is offered in the promise of the gospel. For this reason, we must labor to ensure that the word of God's grace is rooted and grounded in our hearts by faith. It is all one to believe in Christ and to believe the Word that reveals Christ to us. "He who rejects Me, and does not receive My words, has that which judges him—the word that I have spoken will judge him in the last day" (John 12:48). We must, therefore, be like the good ground, which receives and keeps the good seed. It is the word of grace, rooted in our hearts, that keeps us united to Christ, and therefore it is called the "implanted word" (James 1:21). It knits us fast to Christ, and it makes us grow up in Him unto perfection.

We must so esteem and love Christ that, in comparison to Him, we count all things loss and rubbish (Phil. 3:8). We must so delight in Him that we receive nothing into our hearts but Him. Thomas desired to put his finger into Christ's side (John 20:25), but we must go further, and desire to have our souls washed in His blood and our hearts filled with His Spirit.

Christ is the Rock of our salvation, and our hearts must be rooted and founded in Him alone.